Inside A Dog's Mind

Inside A Dog's Mind

Penny For Your Thoughts

* * *

Michelle Holland

Michelle Holland 2020
All rights reserved
No part of this publication may be reproduced, stored in a retrieval system, or transmitted in any form or by any means, without the prior permission in writing of Michelle Holland, nor be otherwise circulated in any form of binding or cover other than that in which it is published and without a similar condition including this condition being imposed on the subsequent purchaser.

THIS BOOK CONTAINS SCENES OF ANIMAL ABUSE AND IS SUITABLE READING FOR ADULTS ONLY

Book cover design by www.samwall. com

I am very proud to be an ISCP dog behaviourist. https://www.insideadogs-mind.co.uk

50% OF ANY PROFIT FROM THE SALE OF THIS BOOK WILL BE DONATED TO DOG RESCUE'S IN NEED OF HELP

Chapter 1

✳ ✳ ✳

"You have to be the most beautiful girl I have ever seen in the whole of my life", says a soft and gentle voice.

I suddenly look up, as I lie shivering on the cold floor of my concrete kennel, and through the old metal prison bars, I see a lady with blonde hair and brown almond shaped eyes smiling down at me.

I immediately jump up and spring into action.

Not many humans have spoken to me in such a gentle manner in the entirety of my life, so I am always grateful for the slightest sign of any kindness shown to me.

"You just want to play with your ball, don't you?" laughs the lady.

For the first time in a long time, I suddenly start to feel happy.

Michelle Holland

I immediately position myself, by crouching down low, and with all the force I can gather, my nose pushes the ball at great speed towards the lady.

I smile to myself as the lady laughs, and I am delighted to see she is now sitting on the concrete step next to my cell.

'I hope her bottom isn't too cold', I think to myself.

I am used to spending twenty-four hours a day sitting or lying on this cold and bleak floor, but this kind lady probably isn't.

I watch with delight, as the lady reaches her hand through the bars, retrieves my ball, and rolls it back to me.

No-one ever plays ball with me and I don't know why. Surely humans know, us border collies constantly want to play.

Back to the job in hand.

I focus on my grubby old tennis ball and once again get myself into position.

'One, two, three', I say to myself, as I push the ball towards the prison bars once again.

"How clever are you?" grins the lady, as we continue to play.

I am in my element and never want this moment to end.

From out the corner of my left eye, I see one of my so-called carers about to walk past. I can't help myself and immediately go into protective mode. I don't want her hurting my new kind human like she does to me. I growl fiercely and show my teeth, as I lunge directly at the prison bars.

"Nutter", I hear the horrible and miserable carer grunt.

"Hey Penny Pops, what on earth is the matter?" my kind human is asking me.

It is times like now, I wish I could speak the human language. I look up into her eyes. She smiles back, as our eyes meet, and for the first time in a long time, I feel a soft and gentle hand stroking my chest.

"There you go. That's better isn't it, my baby?" she continues. "What on earth was all that about?"

I lean my body as close to the bars as I possibly can. This kind and wonderful human touch is somehow pumping endless love directly into my heart. I have never felt so warm and fuzzy. To be honest, I am feeling slightly confused, as I never imagined I could feel something so wonderful. My life has always been hard, lonely and a fight for survival.

"There Penny Pops, that's better isn't it? You like this don't you?" she is asking me in a whisper like voice.

I continue to push my body harder against the bars as I try to get even closer to her.

Michelle Holland

Out of the corner of my eye, I suddenly see my horrible carer walking towards us. I immediately jump up, move backwards, purse my lips, show my teeth, and growl as loudly as I can.

My new lady looks a tad surprised and I watch as she stops the carer in her tracks.

"What is the story on Penny?" I hear her ask, as I continue to growl in a very deep voice.

I watch worriedly as my horrible carer slowly raises one hand towards my new lady. I lunge at the bars at the speed of lightning. I'm having flash backs about the numerous times she has raised her hands to me, and I can assure you, it really hurts.

I feel useless and frustrated not being able to escape from this prison cell to protect my new lady.

'Where have they both gone?' I wonder to myself, as I anxiously look around.

I can hear their voices, but I can't see either of them.

"She is a total headcase. Came in from Ireland after being in a road traffic accident. We rehomed her, she was returned the next day and has been here ever since. That was over three months ago, but not for much longer though", I hear my horrible carer smirk.

"What do you mean? Have you found her a home?" I hear my new lady ask.

"New home? Ha-ha very funny. Who on earth would want to take on a nutcase like her? On Monday morning at nine am, she is booked in to be PTS. Good riddance to bad rubbish, I say", laughs my horrible carer.

'I haven't a clue what PTS means. Maybe, proper training something?' I ask myself.

"You have got to be kidding right? I am not having any of this. Who is in charge here today?" my new lady demands sounding very angry.

"Jess is. Why? What's it got to do with you?" grunts my horrible carer.

"This is totally unacceptable, that's why", replies my new lady.

All that follows is silence.

I feel all alone once again. I listen to the muffled barking and howling from my neighbouring dogs who are also stuck in this demoralising prison. I slowly take a drink from my water bowl and lie down feeling confused.

Where has my new lady gone? Is she ever going to come back? What is going to happen to me on Monday?

My head is whirling with so many questions.

I am feeling very scared, insecure and emotional.

I try as hard as I can but cannot stop the single tear which has been threatening, from rolling down my face.

Chapter 2

✶ ✶ ✶

I HAVEN'T EVEN HAD A walk today. I cannot tell you how miserable I'd felt earlier as different volunteers arrived to take out my prison mates for their daily hour of exercise.

What about me?

Can you believe, all I had earlier this morning was a dried biscuit meal and I have spent the last five hours pacing endlessly up and down my concrete room.

Different humans and their families visit daily where I live. They constantly stare at me through my jail bars. To be honest it makes me feel very uncomfortable. Sometimes I can't control my frustration and end up growling at them. I show off my very white teeth, and it doesn't take them long before they quickly move away.

Every day I watch some of my prison mates leave to start a brand-new life with their new human families.

When will it be my turn?

"Hey Penny Pops, it's me. I am back to see you baby girl", I suddenly hear my kind human's voice say.

I let out a very high-pitched woof in excitement, before picking up my old tennis ball and dropping it next to her welcoming hand by the prison bars.

"You just want to play and play, don't you?" she laughs, as she once again sits down on the cold concrete step.

'Woof', I reply, wagging my tail, as I race off to retrieve my ball.

"I'll stay and play with you for another ten minutes, but I then need to get back to see my own two rescues and our little foster dog. Don't worry though, I promise I will come back to see you tomorrow, if that is ok with you?" she is asking me.

'Is that ok with me? It is more than ok', I say to myself, as I stare into her beautiful brown eyes.

"Now that should have tired you out a little", she tells me, after our ten minutes of priceless fun sadly comes to an end.

I immediately drop the ball and lean my body against the bars trying to get as close to her as I possibly can.

Her hand gently strokes my chest and I have that warm and fuzzy feeling once again. I so wish this kind lady was my regular carer, as she seems to understand me.

"I have never seen a collie so stunning as you Penny Pops. Just look at your long flowing red coat, your soft white chest and your four white socks. I love your beige eyebrows and the little white tip on the top of your red tail too. You could win so many beauty contests. I find you truly mesmerising and beautiful", she continues to tell me, in a very soft voice.

'Wow, no-one has ever said anything this nice about me ever', I think to myself, suddenly feeling emotional.

"Right baby girl, I will be back to see you tomorrow. Love you", she tells me, as she slowly gets up to leave.

No-one has ever told me that they love me before either.

'Please don't go, please stay', I plead, as I start to get myself in a frenzy.

'She has gone', I tell myself feeling lost and alone once again.

In my anger, I pick up the old towel from the back of my cell. I vigorously shake it around to the left and to the right. I spin my body around, come to a halt and tear at the material until I hear the ripping sound. I continue to shred the towel, until my mission is complete.

I wee and poo at the back of my concrete cell, directly on top of the ones I did earlier.

I don't like weeing and pooing where I live, but if no-one takes me out, what else am I supposed to do?

It hasn't always been like this.

One very nice family used to come and take me out for walks quite often. The man was very tall, but also very strong. He had two human puppies, a boy and a girl who were always laughing. They were always so pleased to see me. We would walk around the local field. I'd receive lots of delicious treats and the odd pat on my neck here and there. Occasionally the man would sit on the old wooden bench and tell stories to his human puppies.

To be honest these are the only handful of good times I can remember, apart from today of course.

I am suddenly brought out of my happy daydream, by the sound of the old rattling food trolley, as it slowly makes its way to each prison cell.

I jump up and down in excitement, barking as loudly as I possibly can. I cannot tell you how hungry I am. It seems such a long time ago since breakfast. The prison is filled with different tones of excited barking and howling, as one by one we eagerly wait for our dinner to be served.

Michelle Holland

I groan and growl, as I see my horrible carer approach with a scoop of dry old biscuits.

"Back, back", she is shouting at me, as I watch her struggle to unlock my prison door.

'Grrrrrrr', I tell her, as I crouch down low and bare my teeth.

I stay as low to the ground as I can and closely watch her every move. I cower as her body leans towards me

"Back off now, you horrible, nasty dog", she growls at me, as she tries to throw my dinner into the old metal food bowl.

Most of the biscuits have landed onto the floor. She hurriedly scutters out of my cell and locks me in.

I stay where I am continuing to growl until I know the coast is clear. My horrible carer has hurt me so many times and I cannot forgive her. She has almost choked me by yanking constantly on the heavy metal chain collar which always sits around my neck. I remember gasping for my breath and coughing, but she didn't stop. She wouldn't let me sniff, she just kept pulling me along on what should have been my hourly walk of enjoyment.

One stressful day I won't ever forget, is when she was trying to tidy up my cell and trod on one of my paws with her big heavy boot. I'd instantly yelped out in pain and growled angrily at her. She immediately turned around and hit me in my ribs with the bristle end of her sweeping brush before pinning me harshly against the cell wall whilst clenching her dirty teeth. She continued to laugh at me, as I constantly cried out in pain.

Thankfully, not all the carers are as horrible as she is. I don't have anyone special in my life anymore, that is until today, when the kind lady came to see me.

I crunch on the hard, dry biscuits which always make my mouth feel so dry. I walk across to my water bowl and continuously drink in a bid to help wash them down.

"What a busy body that Jo is. Who does she bloody well think she is waltzing in here demanding a meeting with our manager tomorrow about that nasty Irish dog? She needs to keep her bloody nose out of our business" I suddenly hear my horrible carer say.

"I think that is a being a bit harsh Sharon. I like Penny. How would you feel being locked up for twenty-three to twenty-four hours a day? She is an intelligent border collie and needs plenty of exercise and mental stimulation. No wonder she is going stir crazy", I hear another voice reply.

"Well good riddance to her on Monday", that's all I can say.

Michelle Holland

"Have you not got a heart Sharon? No wonder your nickname around here is the angel of death. Do you know what? I have had enough of this. You are supposed to be involved in rescue because you care about the animals and their welfare, not just condemn them. Each one needs to be listened to as an individual. I will sort out Penny's kennel tonight and tomorrow, but I am telling you now, after that, I quit. I have had more than enough of you and I cannot be around cold-hearted people like you anymore. I don't know how you sleep at night", I hear the other carer blurt out in a very angry voice.

"Good riddance to you too Claire, I will be glad to see the back of you and that bloody dog", I hear my horrible carer reply sarcastically.

Chapter 3

* * *

I AM FEELING VERY CONFUSED.

What is really going to happen to me on Monday?
Why is my horrible carers nickname the angel of death?

"Good girl Penny. I am glad to see you have eaten all of your dinner. I just need to come in and quickly wash down your kennel, clear up the shredded towel which I must say you have done a good job with, grab you a new blanket and make it all nice and comfy for you. Is that ok? I'll just grab a lead, so I can move you into an empty kennel for now", says carer Claire, in a kind soft voice.

I like Claire, she has a wonderful and calm energy. When she walks me, she lets me play ball and encourages me to sniff.

Why can't everyone be like Claire and my new lady?

"Good girl", Claire tells me, as she gently clips the lead onto my chain.

Michelle Holland

"Come on, this way", she encourages me, with a tasty chicken treat.

I look around my new empty cell. Through the bars to my left lies a whippet type of dog, who is fast asleep, in a very cosy looking bed.

Why can't I have a bed like that?

Through the bars to my right, I can see two older looking terrier types. They are lying on a very comfy looking duvet and have a heater above them to keep them warm.

How lucky are they?

Why can't I have a cell like theirs?

Opposite me, I can see a golden retriever dog. He or she has loads of toys to play with.

Why can't I have lots of toys too? All I have is a soggy old ball.

For a slight moment I start to feel sorry for myself and very down in the dumps.

I can hear my horrible carer speaking in the distance. I quickly get ready to lunge at her as she walks past my cell. I bark as loudly as I can, and grab hold of one of the metal bars firmly in my teeth.

She immediately stops, puts her hands on her hips and glares at me with pursed lips.

Inside A Dog's Mind

I let go of the bars, crouch low and continue to bare my teeth at her whilst growling in the deepest voice I can find.

I watch as she slowly makes her way towards me.

I stay focussed on her and continue to growl, as I take two steps backwards.

Her face is between two of the bars. Her lips are still pursed, and she has an evil look in her eyes. Her head suddenly moves, then her mouth opens, and she makes a very strange noise, as some sort of liquid shoots out of her mouth. I feel something land on my back.

"Sharon I cannot believe what you just did. I saw every second of that. You are horrible and disgusting. How low can you go? Spitting at Penny like that is totally unacceptable. I will be putting in a complaint immediately to the committee about your terrible attitude and disgraceful behaviour", bellows Claire, appearing out of nowhere.

"Oh Claire, do whatever you want. They won't listen to you, as you are quitting, remember?" smirks Sharon, in a very sarcastic manner.

"You had better get out of my way now, before I do something I might regret", replies Claire, in a very angry voice.

I have never heard Claire speak in such an angry way.

Sharon takes two steps towards Claire with a big grin on her face. This situation is worrying me, and I quickly spring into action, barking and lunging forward as fiercely as I can at the metal bars.

I need to protect Claire from this monster, but how can I when I am stuck in this cell, feeling useless?

"Sharon, please move out of my way now. I will not ask you again", says Claire, whose face looks to have changed a different colour.

I hold my breath and sigh with relief, as Sharon decides to back off out of Claire's personal space and eventually turns to walk away in the opposite direction.

"A bloody good riddance to both of you", Sharon bellows.

"Oh Penny, I am so sorry that just happened to you. What an evil woman she is, and I will promise you now, I'll make sure she gets punished for her shameful behaviour. Give me two minutes to finish off your kennel, and I'll come back with some wipes to clean that disgusting spit off you", says Claire, who thankfully seems to be calming down at last.

I bark at her and she turns to smile at me.

"Why are you so misunderstood Penny? If I wasn't working such long hours every day, I would take you home with me", she says, with great sadness in her voice.

"Here we go Penny", she continues, as I feel her wiping that liquid stuff from off my back.

"That's better. Now that you are all cleaned up, I'll take you back to your nice clean kennel. I've filled up your bowl with fresh water, and I have managed to find a nice duvet for you too. Much nicer and warmer than that old towel they expect you to sleep on. I can see you have a couple of sores on your elbows from lying on that cold concrete floor, bless you", she tells me.

Oh, how I wish I could go and live with Claire.

"I also saw on the rota, that you haven't even been out for a walk today. For some reason you are on staff walks only and I don't know why, but I will make sure I find out. I promise I will take you out for a nice long walk tomorrow. I'm going to try and get hold of Jo's mobile number when I have finished here. I'll text her to find out what time she is coming tomorrow. Maybe I could ask her if she'd like to join us? Would you like that?" she continues.

'Woof', I respond, as I start to feel happier at last.

"Look at your new bed Penny. Hopefully you'll feel a lot cosier and be able to get a good night's sleep now. As all the others have gone home, I am going to try and find you some toys to play with. I cannot believe you only have that grubby old ball", she smiles, before disappearing.

I look around my clean cell and smile to myself as I make my way over to check out the cosy looking duvet which is sitting against the back wall.

It feels soft to my paws and bouncy too. I sniff it all over. I can smell other dog's scents on it, but I don't care if it is second hand, as this is pure luxury to me.

"Look what I have found", says Claire, as she appears once again, with a huge smile on her face.

I cannot believe it, she is holding a cuddly teddy bear, a large bouncy ball and a giraffe!

"Here we go Penny, meet your new cell mates", she laughs, as she unlocks the door and brings them towards me.

She gently places them down onto my new bed.
How lucky am I?

I feel her hand gently stroking the top of my head.

"Sweet dreams Penny, and I will see you in the morning", she whispers, as she makes her way towards the door.

'Woof', I tell her.

She locks my door and turns to smile at me. A warm and fuzzy feeling is running throughout the whole of my body. I sigh with contentment, as I hold my new Teddy close to me.

I feel snug and warm against my Teddy, and I slowly close my eyes. I try hard to think back to my earliest puppyhood memories.

Chapter 4

* * *

My Mum was a working dog on a farm in the South of Ireland.

Sadly, I never knew my Dad, but Mum said he was one of the best herding dogs around and that me and my siblings should be very proud of him.

I have three sisters and one brother, and we were born and raised in an old hay barn. Once we were old enough to eat solid food, Mum had to return to work, so we all had to learn to fend for ourselves.

We all felt sorry for our Mum, as she used to come home completely shattered after a hard day's work from rounding up the sheep. Her tongue would always be hanging out and her panting would be uncontrollable. She would even be too tired to play with us, and usually just wanted to eat and sleep, trying to give her body time to recover ready for the next working day ahead.

Mum didn't get any time off either. A human man who we rarely saw, would whistle and call out her name at first light. Mum would immediately obey his command and once again we would be left to our own devices.

My brother was very bossy. He enjoyed trying to order me and my sisters around. He'd also try to pinch our breakfast and dinner if we gave him half a chance.

Every morning, a little old human lady would appear. She always looked scraggly and dressed in old rag clothes. Her face was wrinkly, her hair was grey, and she carried this long stick thing when she walked. She didn't stay with us for too long, only enough time to feed us and then she would hobble off out of our barn and wouldn't return until the evening.

One day, our lives were about to change forever.

The human man appeared in our barn one afternoon, but Mum was nowhere to be seen. This was the first time, any of us had seen him this close-up.

He was very tall, rugged looking and wore a flat hat. To me and my siblings he'd looked like a giant. I remember him sitting on a hay bale and picking us up one by one. Next, he looked inside our ears, checked our mouths and teeth and examined our bodies all over. His eyes were very squinty looking, and his hands felt cold, dry and rough against my skin.

Once he'd finished, he whistled loudly, called the name Bessie and our Mum had appeared from out of nowhere.

We were so happy to see Mum, as we never usually saw her during daytime, so this was a very rare occasion indeed.

Mum had asked us to follow her and as usual we immediately obliged. The man walked ahead of us, and suddenly we arrived outside this brick building. A door creaked as it opened, and I was very surprised to see our little human lady standing there.

This building smelt totally different to our hay barn. A musty smell filled the air and there was this very weird material covering the floors, which felt very strange against my paws. I remember looking up to see a fire burning in the wall, it was crackling loudly, and it scared me. I'd jumped backwards feeling very unsure, but Mum had assured me everything was ok. This new place was a lot warmer than what we'd been used to though, so it came as a bit of a shock to our systems.

"That my girl Bessie. You know the ropes only too well. It's time for your puppies to start their training", announced the human man.

Inside A Dog's Mind

Mum had sat us all down and explained that another man called Brian would be coming in to see us once a day to train us. He would be seeing if any of us would be good enough to make the grade and get the fabulous opportunity to be a working sheep dog alongside Mum.

This had sounded very exciting. Of course, my brother thought he would be the one who would shine out brightly from us all.

My sisters and I all agreed, to try our hardest and give him a run for his money.

From that very day we all continued to live inside the house with Mum and the two humans. We were even fed inside too. I even began to like and get used to the warm flames from the fire in the wall. Mum had told us that every time we needed to go to the toilet, we must tap our paw against the wooden door to be let out.

One time, I did feel very sorry for my brother. He'd been asleep and had only just woken up. He'd suddenly darted over to the door and started tapping his paw, but no-one was around to hear him. I know he tried to hold on for as long as he possibly could, but in the end, he didn't have a choice and piddled on the weird material beneath him.

Michelle Holland

When the human man appeared with Mum, he'd got very angry with my brother, and me and my sisters cowered in the corner, as we watched him rub my brother's nose into his own wee.

How terrible is that?

My brother had cried, and I'd noticed tears in Mums eyes too, as the human continued to bellow at him.

Human Brian turned out to be quite a fun and kind human. Every day he would come and spend about an hour with us, and it wasn't too long before we could all sit, give him our paw, and lie down on command. Mum was very proud of us and said we were now moving onto stage two of our training.

One day, Brian informed us that one by one he would be taking us out to meet some sheep. My brother went first, and my sisters and I sat anxiously waiting for him to return.

Brian was smiling when they eventually arrived back and kept telling my brother what a great job he had done. Not long after, it was my turn.

This was all very bizarre to say the least. Brian attached a lead to my collar, and we started to walk across this beautiful green field. There were thousands of smells I desperately needed to investigate, and I continuously found it hard to concentrate on what he was asking of me. I wasn't impressed when I saw these three bundles of wool with thin legs walking towards me. I'd immediately panicked and tried to run away, but the collar was tightening against my throat. I needed to escape from these furry monsters and began yelping as the pain in my neck became excruciating.

"Put them back in the pen", Brian ordered to the human man who we lived with.

He'd whistled and shouted out, "Bessie come bye, away to me, cast, hold, lie down".

I cannot tell you how relieved I'd felt watching Mum spring into action to save me from those walking balls of wool. I'd watched in awe as Mum rounded them safely back into a pen.

"Come on my girl", Brian had said to me, as we slowly made our way back towards the house.

My brother had laughed at me when I told him what had happened. Sadly, my sisters didn't do very well either.

The day after this, a new chapter in our lives was about to begin.

Little did I know, this would be the last time I would ever see my Mum and brother again.

Chapter 5

✶ ✶ ✶

"Come on you four", Brian had said, looking down at me and my three sisters.

I remember feeling very confused, as this morning our brother had gone off to work with Mum.

One by one we were put into this metal thing on wheels. We were quite high up, and through the window we could see Mum and our brother in the distance. A noise made us all jump, and suddenly this thing we were in started bumping around and moving in the opposite direction to where Mum was. We'd tried to keep looking for her, hoping that at any moment she would come and round up this scary metal thing and take us all back home.

The four of us had sat huddled together, shaking with fright.

What was happening to us? Where were we going?

Eventually we came to a halt and in the distance, we could hear muffled barks, but couldn't work out where they were coming from.

One by one Brian lifted us out of the metal thing and handed our leads to a strange human lady.

"Yes Jan. Unfortunately, they all failed the grade. Shouldn't be hard to rehome them though. They're six months old and know all the basic commands. Take good care of them", he'd said to her, before jumping back into the metal thing without even a backward glance.

'Come back Brian. We need to go home to Mum', I'd tried calling out, but sadly he'd already vanished out of sight.

Me and my sisters were taken into this very noisy building. The noise was so loud compared to what we had been used to, as dogs were crying, howling and barking so loudly. My ears had immediately started to hurt.

We were placed in this concrete cell, Jan turned a key and left us there. Suddenly the four of us found ourselves locked in and with no way of escaping.

What was happening to us?

That night as we'd laid on an old damp towel, we'd huddled together crying for our Mum.

Michelle Holland

The next morning, we were given some food and had a chance to look around through the metal bars that surrounded us.

Out of nowhere a tall lady with dark brown hair had suddenly appeared alongside Jan.

"I'll take that one", she'd said, pointing at one of my sisters.

We watched as Jan unlocked the door, put a lead onto our Jess and took her away.

Jess didn't come back and sadly we never saw her again.

To say me and my two remaining sisters were upset, is an understatement. Not only had our sister been taken away, we couldn't understand why we weren't allowed to go home to our brother and Mum? We'd huddled together in our sadness.

That afternoon a human man came and took us out for a walk. The field was heaving with so many different dogs, all playing and having fun. We enjoyed the precious time out of our prison cell, and we were even allowed to sniff and play with some of the other dogs.

One dog who was enormous and funny, told me he was an Irish Red Setter, and when he ran, he bounded along like a thoroughbred. I was having great fun darting under his legs, but on one occasion I completely mistimed my moves, caught one of his back legs by accident and we both ended flat out on top of each other after doing a very impressive roly poly. We were both slightly winded and had laid on the grass laughing until we got our breath back.

Sadly, our playtime came to an end all too quickly. We were taken back inside and once again locked up in our cell. At least we have one Teddy bear between us to keep us company.

My other two sisters Floss and Blossom didn't really join in at playtime. They said the other dogs played too rough and scared them. I did tell them they needed to make the best of the time we were allowed outside, as none of us knew when we would be going back home to our Mum.

The following day, Jan had appeared with an older man and lady at our front door. They seemed very nice people and all three of us wagged our tails, as they offered us tasty treats through the bars.

"It is very hard to choose", the lady had said, in a very soft voice.

'Choose what?' I'd wondered to myself.

"Ok, we will take that one and that one", the man had eventually said, pointing at my two sisters.

Michelle Holland

I remember only too well the panic I'd felt at that precise moment.

I'd watched with tears rolling down my face, as Jan attached a lead onto Floss and Blossom's collar, and they were taken away.

I sat patiently for hours on end waiting for them to return, but they never did. I was feeling truly heart broken. Just little old me and my best friend Teddy left here all on our own with none of our family around.

I'd stifled my cries and snuggled up to Teddy. I prayed Mum would come to find us soon and take me and Teddy back home, where we belonged.

The days, then turned into weeks and sadly nobody came for us. Every day was the same, me and Teddy my best friend in the whole world, stuck on our own, nothing to do apart from play with the few toys we had.

I didn't even see the Red Setter again.

Where had he gone?

I decided I would have to come up with my very own escape plan. I needed desperately to try and find Mum.

Once I had made that decision, I'd felt so much better.

'Tomorrow Teddy, we will be free', I'd told him.

Chapter 6

✶ ✶ ✶

I CAN FEEL MY LEGS continuously twitching, as my eyes open wide.

For a moment, I am confused and cannot get my bearings.

I look down and smile at my Teddy, and it suddenly occurs to me he is not the same one as I used to have when I was younger, you know my best friend.

It takes me quite a while to realise, I had only been dreaming and once again I start to feel sad and lonely

I immediately jump into action and start to bark loudly, as all my cellmates do the same.

Breakfast is on its way.

"Hey there Penny. How did you sleep last night?" Claire asks me, as she unlocks the door and serves my breakfast.

I so wish I could tell her all about my dream. It was like reliving my past, and it just seemed so real being alongside my family once again.

I tuck into my breakfast and it is gone in a flash.

'I wonder what today will bring?' I think to myself.

I am so relieved my horrible carer isn't in today. Every time I see her, I immediately feel angry and for some reason she always makes my blood boil.

"Come on Penny, let's go for a little walk whilst the helpers tidy up your kennel", smiles Claire, as she attaches a lead onto my collar.

I rush to grab Teddy. There is no way I am going to let anyone take my new friend away.

I pee on my favourite patch of grass and follow Claire onto the green field.

"Let's walk this way", Claire tells me, as she points to a bench in the far distance.

I am sure I can see a human sitting on it, but I cannot make out who it is just yet.

I decide to use my nose and lift it high up into the air. Teddy's legs are dangling underneath my throat and I can vaguely hear Claire laughing.

I have a scent and a good one at that.

Taking Claire completely by surprise, I drop Teddy and set off at full pelt across the field.

I cannot feel any pressure on my neck at all, as I run as fast as I can towards the bench.

My nose was right, my kind lady Jo is waiting for me with her arms wide open.

My excitement levels are at the highest. I cannot believe she came back.

How awesome is this?

My body is wriggling ten to the dozen. Jo continues to stroke me, as she tries to calm me down. She is on her knees next to me and I cannot resist giving her a kiss. She laughs as my wet slobbery tongue licks her face.

"I am so happy to see you too Penny Pops", she tells me, with a huge grin across her face.

"Hi Jo. Wow, how clever is Penny? She smelt your scent from a long way away and even dropped her new Teddy, before flying across to you at one hundred miles an hour. I had no chance of holding onto her. She was like a rocket", stutters a very out of breath Claire.

"Isn't she just so clever and beautiful?" beams Jo.

"Sadly, I think there are only the two of us who agree on that one", laughs Claire.

I pick up Teddy and drop him onto Jo's lap.

"Hi Teddy bear", she coos.

"Hold on. Let me take her lead off. I am one thousand percent sure she will not go anywhere whilst the two of us are here with her. She is totally focussed, and I trust her", smiles Claire.

"Ready, steady, go", says Jo, as she throws Teddy across the field.

I spring into action, chase after Teddy, pick him up as gently as I can and race back across to Jo, once again dropping him into her lap.

"Good girlie", praises Jo, as she continues to throw my Teddy.

After repeating this for around at least twenty times, I start to feel tired and drop Teddy down by Jo's side.

"Aw baby. Have we worn you out?" smiles Jo, as she zips open a rucksack.

I am so thirsty and in desperate need of a drink.

"Look what I brought for you", grins Jo, as I watch with delight as she pulls out a plastic dog bowl and a large bottle of fresh water.

'Wow, is Jo a mind reader?' I say to myself, as I lap up the fresh cold water.

I accidently splash the water over Jo's trousers and feel bad.

Jo just giggles.

"Don't you worry about a bit of water Penny Pops. It will soon dry", she assures me.

I am totally speechless. I cannot believe Jo can read my mind.

How cool is this?

"Look at what else I brought for you", she smiles, as she reaches deep down inside her rucksack.

I sit and watch feeling intrigued, as I continuously pant whilst trying to get my breath back.

"Now this is my little magic tin Penny Pops, and do you know what is in here?" she asks me.

My nose is immediately high in the air, as I lean towards the so-called magic tin.

'Chicken, I can smell chicken', I say to myself, as I try hard to stop the dribble escaping from my mouth.

"Looks like you have guessed", laughs Jo, as I dribble even more, as she slowly opens the tin.

The aroma is far too much for me to cope with, and I hold out one paw in hope.

"Oh wow, good girl Penny, I didn't know you could do paw", beams Jo.

"Me neither", replies Claire.

'Delicious', I say to myself, as I gently take the treat Jo is offering me.

"Now, can you do down?" Jo asks me.

'Of course, I can', I say to myself, as I immediately lie down.

"Very impressive Penny", grins Jo, as I get another tasty reward.

"Ok that's enough for now", laughs Claire.

"Why don't you just relax, whilst Claire and I have a little chat?" Jo asks me.

I lay down on the grass with my head on Jo's lap and close my eyes, as I listen to their conversation.

Chapter 7

* * *

"Well Claire. I have a meeting with her this afternoon. Apparently, she needs to get the approval of the committee. I have told her if she dares to go through with the nine o'clock appointment tomorrow, I will make the biggest stink ever and even get the local press involved. Don't you worry Claire, trust me I am standing my ground on this one, and I will not back down. Every dog deserves a second chance, it is as simple as that", I hear Jo's voice say.

"Good on you", replies Claire.

"Becky couldn't believe it when I got home yesterday. She'd asked me how I had got on settling in the new arrivals, and at that point I sobbed my heart out, I couldn't help it", continues Jo.

"What did Becky say?" asks Claire.

"She told me I had to fight for what I believe in, and if we can foster her, then somehow we will", Jo replies.

"What did she say when you told her about the appointment they have booked in for her tomorrow, you know PTS?" I hear Claire ask.

"She was livid and nearly broke down too. She told me to call the manager asap which I did last night and to get an urgent meeting booked in. I totally have her support and one hundred percent backing. I know we have our other three to think about and consider, but she deserves a chance too after what she has been through", says Jo.

I must say I am a tad confused. Surely this proper training something, can't be that bad?

I don't like the idea of Jo crying and I wonder who Becky is?

I look up into Jo's big brown eyes and she stares back into mine. I have never felt such a connection like this before, it feels like we are one. Once again, the warm and fuzzy feeling is rushing through every part of my body and I love it.

Maybe this is what true love feels like?

"Come on Penny, it is time to get you back", says Claire.

Inside A Dog's Mind

I don't want to go back to my cell. I want to stay here feeling fuzzy and warm.

Jo's sighs, "Come on Penny Pops, let's have another little play with your bear on the way back".

I immediately spring into action and pick up Teddy and throw him up into the air. He lands by Jo's foot and they both start to laugh.

"What a great throw Penny. Is there no end to your talents?" laughs Claire.

I stoop my body very low to the ground and get ready for action.

"Ready, steady go", shouts Jo, as Teddy suddenly starts to fly at great speed high up into the air.

I race after him as fast as I can. I come to an immediate halt, look up, put all my weight on my back legs and thrust myself high up into the air to catch him safely.

"Oh, wow Penny Pops, that was truly awesome", beams Jo, as I drop Teddy at her feet.

"Ok, you can have one more go, and then I really must head off home, as Becky, Jacob, Daisy and Honey will be wondering where I have got to, but don't worry I will be back to see you later", smiles Jo, as she gets ready to throw Teddy once again.

'I wonder who Jacob, Daisy and Honey are?" I ask myself, as I rush off to retrieve Teddy.

"Right then Jo, text me later and I will meet you back here with Penny after your meeting", says Claire.

'Did I hear right? I cannot believe I will see Jo again later', I say to myself with a huge feeling of happiness and delight running through every single part of my body.

How cool is this?

"As you know Jo, after yesterday's incident with Sharon, I am quitting, but I am going to wait until I know Penny is safe before I tell them", continues Claire.

"Nice one Claire and thank you", replies Jo.

"Hey Penny Pops", says Jo, as she kneels directly in front of me.

"Now promise me you will be a good girl and behave yourself. I will be back to see you and Claire later this afternoon", she continues, looking directly into my eyes.

That warm and fuzzy feeling is gently throwing through the whole of my body once again.

I hold out my paw, and she smiles at me warmly. She leans forward and gently plants a kiss on my head.

I feel so happy.

"Remember Penny Pops, I love you", she continues, as she slowly stands up.

I am sure I can see tears in her eyes. I hope they are tears of happiness

Jo turns to walk away, and I immediately whine and let out a single woof.

She turns and smiles lifting one hand up and waves it at me.

"Come on, time to get you back for now", says Claire.

An overwhelming feeling of sadness engulfs me, and I keep looking back for Jo, but she is nowhere to be seen.

It isn't long before we are back in my cell. I am thankful I have Teddy to cuddle up to.

I continue to pace as I wait patiently for Jo or Claire to return.

Where are they?

Chapter 8

✷ ✷ ✷

"Hey Penny. It's me again, do you fancy another walk", grins Claire, as she suddenly appears holding a lead.

'Do you really need to ask?' I think, as I rush to pick up Teddy.

"Aw, that is so sweet Penny, you love your new bear, don't you?", laughs Claire, as the three of us make our way out of the prison and into the glorious fresh air for the second time today.

Two walks in one day, I cannot believe it.

Off we go down the concrete steps, around the corner, down the next flight and onto my favourite patch of grass.

I have a quick wee, before we move on.

One thing us dogs need to get used to in prison is number one, we have no choice but to go to toilet

Inside A Dog's Mind

in the cell where we live. Number two, we wear these awful chain collars around our necks twenty-four hours a day, and as the lead tightens when we get too excited, they really hurt our throats. The other annoying thing about wearing them, is that they jingle every time you move. Us collies have very sensitive hearing, and the constant metal touching metal can sometimes hurt our ears, surely humans know this? *Maybe not.*

"Come on Penny, this way", Claire encourages me, as we head towards the field.

I can hear a very familiar voice calling my name.

'I cannot believe Jo is back', I call out, as I nearly pull Claire over, as she tries to hang onto me.

"Hey Penny Pops", she grins, as I race into her arms, still holding Teddy whilst my body continues to dance around in excitement.

"Hi Teddy", she laughs, as I throw him at her feet.

"Come on, let's go for a walk and you can tell me how your meeting went. I have been feeling on edge worrying about everything", says Claire, as she unclips my lead.

I feel like jumping with glee, we are the only ones here. We have this fabulous field all to ourselves.

"You won't believe what she said Claire", says Jo.

"Please tell me", she pleads.

Michelle Holland

"Well, can you believe her first question to me was, Jo why do you want to save Penny? Why don't you adopt or foster one of the other foreign dogs instead? I'd replied in a very stern voice, because Penny is on my doorstep and she deserves a chance to have a happy life too. I then asked her who had made the decision to have Penny PTS and she told me it was the kennel staff. Can you believe this Claire?" Jo replies.

"I bet this is all down to the angel of death", says Claire shaking her head angrily.

"My next question to her was how could she be labelled as aggressive, when she hasn't actually bitten anyone? She told me she'd lunged at Sharon fiercely, baring her teeth and growling at her. I replied, well that's understandable, as I want to lunge at Sharon every time, I see her too", Jo continues.

"You didn't?" laughs Claire.

"Blooming right I did! I also asked her, as she is the manager how much time had she personally spent with Penny? Her answer was none and then she said, I leave that to my staff to deal with. Honestly Claire my blood was boiling", says Jo.

"Mine is boiling near to overload after what you have just told me", replies Claire.

'This is a very bizarre and weird conversation', I think to myself, as I continue to sniff and listen.

"I told her that I felt it was her responsibility as the manager to assess Penny herself over a period of weeks, not to just condemn her. Why don't you work alongside collie rescues? I'd asked. Her answer was, we don't work with any other organisations, as we prefer to work on our own. I replied, to be honest, I can totally understand why Penny isn't happy. A very intelligent collie pacing up and down a small concrete kennel for twenty-three hours, sometimes twenty-four hours a day for over three months, with strangers continuously staring at her, dogs barking constantly and so many different types of energies all around her. Not an ideal environment for any dog, let alone a border collie", says Jo.

"Well done you for sticking up for Penny and standing your ground", replies Claire.

"I then told her I was totally saddened, as I truly feel that Penny has been failed by the system. As a fully qualified behaviourist with the ISCP, even I can see Penny is suffering from severe kennel stress and anxiety. I would go stir crazy too if I was stuck in her environment for over three months, wouldn't you? Eventually, she said she would speak to the committee and get back to me by tomorrow, and she had the cheek to tell me I couldn't save every dog", continues Jo.

"But what about the appointment she has made? You know the PTS", asks Claire.

"She assured me this would be cancelled until she hears the committee's final decision. I did also inform her, that I wasn't prepared to let this matter drop. I told her we would be happy to foster Penny and do a full assessment on her and if all goes well eventually, rehome her into a suitable environment.", says Jo.

"Nice one Jo. Well I will make sure I'll be here at seven thirty in the morning and I promise you now, I will not let Penny out of my sight", replies Claire.

"Oh no, look at the time. Penny Pops I need to go home now, as I have some work to catch up on ready for tomorrow", Jo suddenly announces.

'But I don't want you to go' I cry out, suddenly getting myself into a bit of a state.

"Ok Jo and thank you for all of your help. I'll take Penny back to her kennel now. Why don't you text me tomorrow as soon as you have heard from her?" says Claire.

"That sounds like a plan. Penny Pops I promise you I will be back to see you tomorrow. Please trust me and don't forget I love you", calls Jo, as she walks off in the opposite direction to us.

I bark and jump around, but Claire takes no notice and soon I am back in my cell with Teddy.

I am totally confused as to what is going on.

I lie on my duvet with Teddy and close my eyes. It isn't long before I drift off into a very deep sleep.

Chapter 9

✶ ✶ ✶

I AM BACK IN THE first prison and today is the day I am determined to escape. Yesterday, I had a good old sniff around the hedges and noticed a gap which I am positive I should be able to squeeze through.

I have gone through the plan so many times in my head and know I need to get this right on the first attempt, as if I mess this up, I will be stuck in here for the foreseeable future.

'Time for your walk Penny', smiles Jan, as she opens my cell door.

I rush to pick up Teddy. I am certainly not going anywhere without him.

"You don't need to bring your Teddy with you", says Jan, as she leans forward to take him from me.

I give her a warning growl.

"Hey, there is no need to growl at me Penny. Ok, come on then, your bear can come with you if you want him too", she says, with a slightly confused look across her face.

I smirk to myself.

"Jan you are needed urgently. Two dogs are kicking off in the field. Let me take that dog off your hands. Quickly Jan, run", says a younger human, with great urgency to her voice.

Jan quickly hands my lead over, and we follow her out to the field.

All hell is breaking loose, and everyone is running around in a mad panic.

"Quickly Sasha, we need your help. Take Penny's lead off and let her go for now. Hurry up", Jan urges.

'This is my golden opportunity", I think to myself, as I casually make my way towards the hedgerow.

'Where is that gap?' I ask myself, as I start to get panicky.

I sniff as hard as I can, with Teddy hanging out from my mouth. I have no choice but to drop him, so I can make proper use of my senses.

'Bingo. Well done Penny', I grin to myself.

I can hear Jan shouting my name. I know I need to make a run for it, but I can't go without Teddy.

Michelle Holland

I dash as fast as I can, gently pick him up, and dart towards the gap like a rocket.

It is a tight squeeze, but we are nearly through.

I can hear Jan's voice getting closer, as I make one final push for freedom.

We are through. I quickly put my nose up high into the air. We need to go left.

Off Teddy and I go at the speed of lightning. We keep running and running without looking back.

Eventually, I come to a standstill and drop Teddy onto the grass whilst I get my breath back.

I cannot believe we have done it.

I feel thirsty after all my exertions and need to find water.

I stand and hold my nose up high into the air and sniff for all I am worth.

'Come on Teddy', I say to him, as I gently pick him up.

We wander down a glorious country lane towards some woodland, and being a country girl, I know I will find some water soon.

The woodland stands tall and proud, but the temperature suddenly drops as we make our way through the temple of trees full of deep green leaves. The sun seeps through now and again, from the branches directly above us.

I suddenly hear voices, and hurry to hide behind a big oak tree. I can hear a family chatting and I stay as still as a statue. I wait patiently until the coast is clear, so Teddy and I can carry on with our mission to find water.

In the distance I can hear the trickle of water. I immediately pick up my pace and follow my nose.

'Bingo', I say to myself, as I see a fresh running stream ahead of me.

I gently drop Teddy to the ground and make my way down towards the stream.

My paws gently touch the cold clear water, and within seconds I lap it up as if there is no tomorrow. I gently lower my body into the stream as far in as I can.

'This feel like heaven', I say to myself, as I dunk my head in too.

I have the urge to lift all four paws off the ground and I haven't a clue why.

Suddenly, I am paddling with all four paws off the ground.

I cannot believe I am swimming! OMG. I didn't know I could swim.

How amazing is this?

This is an awesome feeling and now I feel the happiest I have felt in a very long time.

Michelle Holland

Eventually, I crawl up the bank of the stream and stand in the glorious sunshine, whilst I shake continuously. I can feel droplets of water flying all around me.

What great fun this is.

'Hey Teddy. Did you just see what I did?' I ask him, as I gently pick him up.

He doesn't bother to respond. He has never been very talkative, but I don't care, as he is my best friend and good company too.

I need to find food and shelter.

I think hard to try and come up with a plan.

We continue to wander around the woodland in search of food. I can see many picnic tables with lots of humans chatting with their puppies and I can smell lots of delicious food.

I decide it would be safer to hide away until all the humans have gone home, in the hope that they will leave something behind for me.

Teddy and I make our way deeper into the woods in search of somewhere to sleep. Ahead of us I can see this wooden triangular looking thing, so I decide to go and investigate.

Very interesting, it has three sides and a pointy top. The soil on the base is nice and dry.

'This is pawsome', I think to myself, as I gently lower Teddy into our new home.

An overwhelming feeling of tiredness comes over me. I curl up with Teddy and my eyes start to close.

Chapter 10

✳ ✳ ✳

An owl hooting loudly immediately alerts me and I wake up in a flash. I look all around and I am so relieved to see Teddy is still lying next to me. Everywhere is dark, and my tummy is rumbling badly. I must have been completely exhausted after pulling off my escape plan earlier.

As Teddy doesn't eat at all, I decide to leave him sleeping whilst I head off in search of food.

I slowly follow my nose through the dark woodland. I can hear a rustling noise to my right and glance around to see a grey squirrel hurriedly scuttling away up a nearby tree trunk.

I really don't fancy catching and eating a squirrel tonight, so I carry on following my nose.

Eventually, I arrive back at where the humans were sitting earlier at the picnic tables. All around me looks totally deserted, not a single human in sight.

Inside A Dog's Mind

My nose guides me to a rubbish bin. I jump up on my hind legs to investigate. I can smell egg and cheese coming from somewhere. I lean as far forward as I possibly can. My teeth grab hold of a plastic bag, I lift my head up high and throw it down onto the floor. I sniff around the bag thoroughly and am thrilled to find some leftovers. Half a cheese sandwich, half a boiled egg, a piece of chicken and some funny tasting crisps.

'Better than nothing', I think to myself, as I ensure I eat every available crumb.

Suddenly my tongue feels as though it is on fire and I have the sudden urge to drink water.

I run to the stream as fast as my legs will carry me, nearly falling over a hidden rock. I have never felt so thirsty. I lap the water continuously until the burning sensation eventually subsides.

'What was all that about?' I say to myself, as I head back to find Teddy.

Within seconds, I feel the most excruciating cramps in my tummy and have the sudden urge to do a poo.

'Oh no', I think so myself, as I immediately come to a standstill.

I crouch down as low as I can to get ready to go to the toilet. It takes me completely by surprise as diarrhoea teams out from my bottom. I have no control at all. It won't stop and it smells absolutely disgusting.

Eventually the horrible cramps stop, but I feel totally exhausted and very thirsty once again.

Off to the stream I go, but this time I decide to have a drink and wash my smelly bottom at the same time.

'Phew', I think to myself, as the thirst quenches disappear at last, as I work hard to shake my bottom dry.

I slowly make my way back to Teddy and slump down next to him.

A harsh lesson learned this evening. I will be extra careful about what I find in rubbish bins from now on. I now need to come up with another type of eating plan.

The sound of birds singing wakes me up and I smile as I look across at Teddy. I slowly get up and stretch and let out a very loud gush of wind at the same time. I quickly turn around to check I haven't woken Teddy up.

'He sleeps through absolutely everything', I think to myself with a smile.

I decide to leave Teddy where he is whilst I nip down to the stream for a drink of water. Feeling so much better and totally refreshed after having a quick bath, I head back off to pick up Teddy.

It is time for us to move on.

We slowly make our way through the woodland and head out into the beautiful green countryside.

'This is so much better than being locked in that prison cell', I think to myself.

I have decided it is best if we make our way to one of the main towns, as it should be easier to find food and who knows maybe we could even hitch a lift home to Mum?

The sun is feeling warm on my back, so I decide to take a rest in a shady area by a nearby tree. From my strong sense of smell, I think we still have approximately five miles ahead of us to get to the nearest town.

After a twenty-minute rest, I gently pick up Teddy and we continue on our travels.

Suddenly, I am startled by a group of those balls of wool on thin legs wandering around in a field to my left, so I decide to up my pace sharply.

My tummy is rumbling once again, and I am starting to feel thirsty.

A memory suddenly springs into my head, something Mum once told us. She'd said when she was around two years old, she had been left outside for three whole days and nights, as her humans had rushed away at short notice. They had forgotten to leave her any food or water and she told us how her survival instincts had kicked in. She'd managed to get access to water from drinking out of the troughs in the numerous fields around the farm. Her food came from searching the fields for rabbit droppings, as they apparently contain a rich source of fibre and vitamin b, but she warned us never to eat a dead rabbit as this could give us something called tapeworm and I certainly don't like the sound of that. Mum had also said our natural instincts should tell us which grasses and plants are safe for us to eat too.

I pop Teddy down and take a stroll around an empty field and to my utter delight I am thrilled to find lots of little brown pellets scattered everywhere.

Without any hesitation at all, I turn into a lawnmower and to be honest they don't really taste of anything, but if Mum says they are ok to eat, then I believe her.

The gurgling inside my tummy has finally stopped and at last I am feeling full. I wander around the field until I find an old metal water trough and I jump up to take a peep inside. Apart from a few dead flies floating around, the water doesn't look too bad, so I decide to get stuck in.

Feeling refreshed and refuelled, I head off to find Teddy and our journey continues.

Inside A Dog's Mind

The weather has turned cloudy and it smells like there could be rain on the way, so I quicken my pace.

I need to find us some shelter.

We must be getting close to a town, because I can hear noises not too far away in the distance and the smell of diesel is flying up my nostrils.

I can see an enormous looking building ahead, so I stop to observe from afar.

Suddenly, there is a large bang of thunder, the heavens open and the rain starts to thrash down. I run for cover into an empty shop doorway and curl up as tightly as I can into a ball with Teddy close beside me. There are so many humans rushing towards the big building, whilst laughing and shouting and most are wearing scarfs around their necks.

'How strange', I think to myself.

Many metal things on wheels continue to drive up and down the road, splashing the water high up onto the pavements.

My nose starts to twitch as I smell a delicious aroma, possibly a burger coming from the other side of the road just outside the large building everyone seems to be rushing in to.

My tummy has started to rumble, but I decide to stay where I am and watch safely from a distance.

Michelle Holland

I can hear loud chanting, lots of clapping and whistles blowing from inside the building. My ears are beginning to hurt and my head is starting to pound. I watch a human drop what looks to be a half-eaten burger down onto the ground and my mouth starts to drool with saliva.

'Wait here Teddy', I tell him, as I decide to try and get to it before anyone else does.

I look to my left and to my right, no metal things in sight.

I run as fast as I can towards the burger. The next think I hear is the screech of brakes. An horrific pain shoots through the back of my legs and everything goes black.

Chapter 11

*** * ***

I slowly open my eyes.

Where am I?

There are lots of voices talking, but I can't see anyone at all.

Where is Teddy?

I try to move, but the pain in my left hind leg is excruciating and I feel like I am going to be sick.

"Hey little girl, please try not to move. We are here to help you", says a soft ladies voice, through a green looking mask.

I try hard to remember what had happened to me. I feel a sharp prick in my front left leg, and suddenly my eyes refuse to stay open.

"Why not let us see if we can tempt you with a little bit of chicken? You have been asleep on and off for nearly twenty-four hours. The operation went very well indeed. Luckily for you it was a clean break to your hind tibia bone. We have managed to pin it back together and in eight to ten weeks of taking things easy you should be back to normal and fit and ready to go home", says a young nurse, who is leaning through what looks to be a door to my new house. Thin small wire windows look to be all around me.

'But I don't have a home. I want my Mum', I cry.

She holds out her hand and offers me some chicken.

I slowly try to lift my head, but I'm finding this rather difficult, as I seem to have a plastic lampshade stuck on the top of it.

As gently as I can take the chicken. It tastes so good.

"Good girl. I would love to know where you came from and where your owners are, but unfortunately, we cannot find a microchip. We have put an appeal on our website and circulated a few posters locally to see if anyone comes forward", she continues.

'I hope Teddy comes to find me, as he is my one and only friend', I think to myself feeling sad.

"How is she doing?" I hear a human man's voice ask.

I can't see him. All I can see is a pair of brown shoes and the bottom of his trousers from where I am lying.

"She is doing well John. Her temperature and pulse are completely back to normal", replies the lady.

"That is great news Anna. Keep the pain killers pumping in for today and I will pop by to access her again tomorrow. She really does need a name poor love", he replies.

"Well on my way to work this morning, I found a penny on the pavement which I picked up, as apparently it is supposed to bring good luck", she tells him.

"Penny, it is then", says the man, before disappearing out of sight.

"I hope you like the name I have chosen for you Penny", she tells me, with a very warm smile, as she continues to offer me more chicken.

I blink my left eye at her in agreement.

"Now just you rest for now and I will be back to check on you later", she tells me, before slowly closing my front door.

I slowly move my eyes around to look at my new surroundings. I can't see too much, apart from a large white room in front of me. I have a lovely comfy bed to lie on and my new house has blankets on the top of the roof and on the back and side walls. I do feel comfy and warm although my new house is very small. I feel drowsy and cannot stop my eyes from closing.

"There you are sleepy head", I hear a familiar voice saying, as I slowly open my eyes.

Michelle Holland

My nurse Anna is smiling at me through the little squares.

I watch closely as she opens my front door and offers me more chicken.

'I have never had room service like this before', I think to myself with a smile.

I feel much better for my sleep, and I gobble the chicken down as quickly as I can.

"Well done Penny. I am thrilled to see you have got your appetite back, that is a very good sign", she grins at me.

I wince in pain as I try to stand up. My legs feel slightly wobbly and I don't seem to be able to put one of my back legs onto the floor.

"Steady now Penny. We need to take things slowly, as it is very early days. Do you feel up to a short stroll, so you can have a sniff around and maybe try to go to the toilet?" she asks me.

With all the strength I can gather, I pull myself up and am very pleased to be standing on three legs. For some peculiar reason, my fourth leg, feels heavy and tight. I glance around and notice a dark blue bandage running from the bottom of my paw all the way up to the top of my hip.

"Wait there one second whilst I grab a lead Penny", says Anna, as she disappears out of sight.

Inside A Dog's Mind

Within seconds she is back with a lead and a funny looking long sock thing.

"Now come here whilst I take off your collar. There we go, I bet that feels better doesn't it?" she smiles.

'What a relief to have that lampshade off my head at last', I say to myself.

"Now we have no rush Penny, so just take your time. I will put this stocking underneath your tummy by your back legs for support if needed, because I don't want you putting your poorly leg onto the ground yet, as it is too early for you to weight bear. Right, are we ready to go?" she asks.

I slowly make my way across this very clean looking room on three legs. Anna seems very pleased with my progress as we make our way outside onto a lovely patch of rich looking grass. My nose immediately goes into overdrive, as I start to sniff the various smells all around.

"Steady", says Anna, as I suddenly feel her starting to lift my back legs with the stocking thing, which is sitting under my tummy.

I am desperate for a wee, and Anna laughs at me, as I lean forward on my front legs with my backside high into the air and go to the toilet.

"I didn't know you could do acrobats Penny. What a fabulous way of having a wee without putting any weight on your hind legs. What a clever girl you are", she continues.

I suddenly have the urge to go for a poo. I try to stoop down low, but I am finding the position very uncomfortable and slightly painful.

"Good girl Penny. Don't worry, I will make sure I support your poorly leg", she assures me.

I cannot tell you relieved and happy I feel after doing a poo, and Anna seems elated too. I watch her pull out a plastic bag from her pocket and clear it up in jiffy.

The sun is feeling lovely and warm on my back. It is so nice to be out in the fresh air again and to have the freedom of going to the toilet.

I haven't had much choice other to go on the paper pads that lie underneath me on the bed in my crate since my accident, so this is a big step forward.

"Come on then Penny. Let's get you back inside so you can have a rest", she tells me, as we start to make a move.

I can't believe this little stroll has taken everything out of me and by the time I arrive back at my new house, I am totally shattered.

"I will be back later to change your bandage and take you for another walk. We need to build up your strength slowly", she informs me, as she sticks the lampshade back on my head.

"See you later", she calls, as she closes my door and disappears out of sight.

I cannot stop my eyes from closing. I am completely exhausted.

Chapter 12

* * *

"Good girl", praises Anna, as I retrieve the squeaky giraffe and drop it at her feet.

I look up at her, wag my tail and woof.

"That's enough for today Penny. Your twelve weeks of convalescing is now up, and you are ready to move on to the next part of your journey", she tells me.

'But I quite like it here, in fact I wouldn't mind staying longer until I can find my Teddy and go back to Mum', I try to tell her.

"Come on. We need to get your suitcase packed and ready to go", she smiles.

'Where am I going? I don't want to leave here', I think to myself, with panic starting to erupt.

"Elaine, this is Penny. Thankfully she has fully recovered, and I have all her travel documents ready for you. Make sure you take good care of her, as she

Inside A Dog's Mind

is one special girl", says Anna, to a human lady who looks to be in her forties.

"Don't worry Anna, I'll take good care of her for you", assures Elaine, as Anna hands over my lead.

Anna stoops down and plants a single kiss onto the top of my head.

"Stay safe and have a great life", she whispers, in a slightly broken voice, before turning around to make her way out of the front door.

'But I don't want to go. I want to stay here', I cry to myself, as I stick my paws to the floor, refusing to move.

"Come on Penny. Would a little treat help?" asks Elaine, as she gently coaxes me to walk forward.

'I suppose so', I mumble to myself, reluctantly moving forward.

A huge white metal thing on wheels is waiting for us.

'Maybe I am going home to my Mum at last?' I think to myself, starting to feel slightly more positive.

I jump into the van, and Elaine shuts me inside a crate, just like the one I have been living in recently. I am amazed to see other dogs in houses too and totally surprised to see some cats as well.

'Maybe they are they all coming to live with me and Mum?' I think to myself.

Michelle Holland

Even though it was very warm outside, it is nice and cool in here even with all the windows closed.

Thankfully, I do have a nice soft bed and a bowl of water.

It isn't long before we start to move.

It feels like I have been in here for ages and I desperately need to stretch my legs.

Eventually after what seems days, but is probably only a few hours, we come to a standstill and one by one, we are fed some very tasty food. After I've finished eating, Elaine pops back to put on my lead and I follow her outside to go to the toilet.

The air smells totally different to what I am used to, there is a slight salty taste in my mouth and the temperature seems a lot cooler than earlier. Once I have done my toilet, she takes me back to my little house and closes the door.

I watch intrigued as one by one she takes the others outside, apart from the cats who don't seem to be going anywhere.

Suddenly, we are moving, but within minutes we stop once again, and I can hear lots of strange voices outside.

The side door starts to open, and a strange man is looking in. He seems to be holding lots of little booklets in his hands, as he peers inside and checks our houses one by one.

"Yes, this looks all in order", he says to Elaine, in a very gruff voice.

The door starts to close and they both disappear.

Within minutes we are moving again.

Something feels very strange and different.

We seem to be bobbing up and down and it is starting to make me feel slightly queasy.

I close my eyes, but this doesn't make me feel any better, in fact I feel worse. Everything is dark and eerie.

I swallow, trying hard to avoid being sick.

This has been going on for hours and I don't know how much longer I can hold out.

I cannot tell you relieved I am when the bobbing up and down finally stops, and the metal thing goes back to behaving normally.

The side door opens once again and a human lady is standing next to Elaine, holding those familiar booklets in her hands again.

She peers in, checks us one by one and says to Elaine, "Thank you. Yes, everything is all in order. Please drive down to the right and then take the first left. Have a safe trip".

Michelle Holland

I have never heard a human talk with an accent like this before. She sounds very posh and ladylike.

It isn't long before we come to another halt, and one by one Elaine lets us out for a few minutes of fresh air.

"Welcome to England Penny", she tells me, as I try to regain my balance.

I still feel like I am floating around. How bizarre is this?

Off we go again and thankfully this time we are not bouncing up and down.

I haven't a clue where England is, but I hope I'll see Mum real soon.

We come to a stop after around three hours and Elaine appears at the side door. Four other humans are standing with her.

I watch closely, as they take a Springer Spaniel looking dog out of his house.

"This is Riley, neutered and he has just turned eight months old. He was brought in as a stray", Elaine tells the others, and then Riley vanishes.

"Lilly, is ten months old, not spayed and another stray with no history", she continues, as I watch this small cream whippet type of dog, go off with one of the other humans.

Inside A Dog's Mind

"Charlie is approximately twelve months old, another stray. He isn't neutered and had a bad flea infestation when he was found wandering the streets", says Elaine, as she hands the tiny, skinny looking dog over to another waiting human.

"Last but not least is Penny. She had been involved in a road traffic accident approximately three months ago and has a metal pin in her left hind tibia. Not spayed and no other history, just another stray. Approximate age is around about fourteen months", she says, before clipping on my lead and asking me to follow her out of the metal thing.

I start to panic. I haven't a clue what is happening to me.

"Follow me Penny", says the voice of a smallish human lady.

I can smell lots of other dogs around and decide to have a wee on the grass to mark my territory.

I follow my human up a concrete path and up some steps. We turn right and go up some more steps. In front and to either side of me stand many prison cells full of howling and barking dogs.

'Nooooo, I don't want to be back in prison again, I just want my Mum', I cry out to myself.

"This way", says my human, as she slowly drags me into a cell.

Michelle Holland

'Stop it', I want to shout, as the collar tightens around my neck.

I look around my concrete cell and the metal bars that surround me.

Feeling sad and depressed I curl up on the old towel at the back of my cell.

I close my eyes and pray this is all just a horrible nightmare.

Chapter 13

* * *

I CANNOT SLEEP. THERE IS too much noise going on all around me. This is real and there is nothing I can do about it.

Once again, I have found myself back in prison.

A human brings me a bowl of dried biscuits, which I gratefully gobble down as quickly as I can, and then I don't see any humans until the following morning.

I didn't sleep very well, as one dog cried constantly throughout the night and sounded in a great deal of pain.

My cell mates start to go crazy, as the breakfast trolley rattles by.

I stand and wait patiently, but it doesn't stop at my cell.

'Where the heck is my breakfast? I am starving', I think to myself, feeling very annoyed.

The same human I saw yesterday arrives at my door holding a lead.

Michelle Holland

Maybe she is taking me home to Mum?
I haven't even had a drink yet either.

My lead is on and she bends down to attach a tag like thing onto my collar. We head towards the steps we came up yesterday, around the corner, back down some more steps and arrive at the same piece of grass I weed on yesterday, so I oblige once again.

Lilly and Charlie who arrived with me yesterday are also waiting with their two humans.

I haven't a clue what is happening to us now.

Another metal thing arrives and we all clamber in. We are each put into a tiny house and then suddenly we are moving, but where are we going?

'Hopefully to see my Mum', I say to myself.

It isn't long until we come to a halt and all clamber out.

This is not where my Mum lives? There are so many brick houses stuck together.

"This way Penny", my human says, as we follow Lilly and Charlie through this huge wooden door.

A familiar smell makes me stop in my tracks. It reminds me of when I hurt my leg, but my leg is fine now, so what is going on?

"Penny first", says a lady, who looks like a nurse.

We follow her into a smallish room.

"I will just check her over and listen to her heart to make sure everything is ok and then we can get her sedated", says the nurse.

'What does this mean?' I think to myself, feeling rather apprehensive.

"Yes, she is all good to go", says the nurse.

Fabulous news. I can go home now, right?

Wrong.

I feel a tiny prick in my front right leg and suddenly start to feel woozy. A horrible feeling of tiredness engulfs me, my eyes refuse to stay open, and everything goes black.

"Well done Penny, that's it. Now wake up nice and slowly", I can hear a voice telling me.

Where am I? What is happening?

I open my eyes and they slowly start to focus.

Oh no, I have another plastic lampshade stuck on my head. How on earth did that happen?

Not long after, my other human appears and lifts me off the table I have been lying on.

Ouch, my tummy feels sore. What have they done to me?

I gingerly follow my human into a very large and open area. I am very surprised to see Lilly and Charlie patiently waiting. They both looking groggy too, just how I feel, and they also have lampshades stuck on their heads.

Michelle Holland

It isn't long before we are lifted back up inside the metal thing. My human struggles to get me into my small house as the lampshade keeps banging against the crate. It is a very tight squeeze, but she gets there in the end.

It isn't long before we arrive back at the same piece of grass I weed on earlier. As I stoop down, a sharp pain shoots through the bottom end of my tummy.

Why is it hurting when I wee?

We slowly make our way up the path, up the concrete steps, and round to the left.

I stop as I look at the next set of steps ahead. I am finding this a bit of a struggle.

"Nearly there", says my human, as I gingerly climb the next two steps. My lampshade is making this very difficult for me. I need to keep my head up high enough, to avoid banging it against the concrete steps.

My prison awaits me, and I gingerly lie down on the old towel at the back of my cell feeling, very, very sorry for myself.

I have the same daily routine. Horrible dried biscuits for breakfast, a walk to my favourite piece of grass, have a wee and poo, and back to my cell. Different humans walk up and down the prison for quite a few hours a day. Some stop to read a piece of paper which sits on the outside of my prison bars. Late afternoon, dried biscuits for dinner, a walk to my favourite piece of grass, have a wee and poo, back to my cell. Go to sleep and start all over again.

I cannot believe it has taken all this time for my carers to finally realise I have a lampshade stuck on top of my head, so I am elated when they eventually remove it and at last I can move my head around properly.

I immediately look underneath my tummy and I am shocked to see a two-inch scar.

How on earth did that happen?

I sniff closely and can smell some type of antiseptic.

'What have they done to me? What is all this about?' I think to myself, feeling worried.

Chapter 14

* * *

"Now just look at you, aren't you a very pretty girl", I hear a human lady say.

I look her up and down. She is tall, with grey hair, and looks to be very well dressed.

"Approximately fourteen months old. A stray from Ireland. Needs lots of exercise. Not suitable to rehome with children under the age of twelve. Ask at reception for more details", she continues.

Why is she talking about me like this? I am not a stray. I just need to get home to be with my family. I am sure they are all out searching for me.

Suddenly she disappears, but then ten minutes later she reappears with one of the prison carers at her side.

"Come on Penny. Would you like to go for a walk with Mrs Andrews?" my carer asks me.

'Do I have a choice?' I say to myself.

Inside A Dog's Mind

My lead is on and soon we are making our way down the concrete steps, around the corner we go, another load of steps, onto the path and eventually arrive at my favourite patch of green grass.

I immediately mark my territory in my usual spot and follow them onto the green exercise field.

I can see Charlie and Lilly in the distance, walking with their carer's.

I wonder if they would like to come and play with me?

I start to head off in their direction, but a sudden hard yank from the lead to my collar stops me in my tracks.

'My poor throat', I think to myself, as I gasp for breath.

"Personally, I don't like choke collars. Surely you know they can do a lot of damage to a dog's throat?" blurts out Mrs Andrews.

"We use what we are told to", my carer replies.

"Well, I think they should be banned", continues Mrs Andrews.

Maybe this lady isn't too bad after all?

"Would you like a treat Penny?" asks Mrs Andrews.

Now what a silly question to ask me!

I decide to sit down and offer my paw, and I get rewarded with a nice chicken treat, which I take very gently from her.

"Good girl Penny. How would you feel about coming to live with me?" she asks.

I am not too sure about this.

'I suppose it is better than being in prison and who knows, I could possibly come up with another escape plan?' I think to myself.

"Yes, I will take her with me today. You have already done a home visit, so I assume this whole process should be quite straight forward?" she asks.

"I will take you to reception, so you can fill out the adoption forms. Follow me", my carer replies.

I am going home with this stranger, who I have only just met? This has all come as a bit of a shock to me.

I sit patiently in reception whilst the paperwork is completed. There is one carer that really doesn't like me, and she is standing behind the desk. She keeps glancing over at me and showing her teeth. To be honest she makes my skin scrawl and I always feel on edge when I see her.

I shall certainly be happy to get away from her, that's for sure.

It doesn't take long before I am asked to jump into another metal thing, but this time, I have a harness on which is clipped to a sort of seat belt. I sit on the back seat which I have all to myself. I can even see out of the windows and I am amazed to see such beautiful countryside surrounding me.

Chapter 15

* * *

Around twenty minutes later, we pull up at this old looking cottage and my new carer unclips my seatbelt.

"Come on Penny, follow me. It is time for you to meet your brother and sisters", she tells me.

I seriously cannot believe it.

She has found my family, but what about Mum? She didn't mention her at all.

I am feeling nervous but excited about seeing my siblings again.

"Right, in we go Penny", she tells me, as we walk through the front door into a very large hallway.

I put my nose high into the air and sniff for all I am worth. I cannot smell my siblings anywhere which is very weird, as I do have an amazing and strong sense of smell.

I am very confused.

Michelle Holland

"This way", she tells me, as she unclips my lead and opens another door.

I wait eagerly in anticipation for my siblings to appear.

"Penny, meet Foxy, Lucy and Dora", she tells me, with a huge grin on her face.

I am rooted to the spot in shock.

'These are not my siblings. They are cats', I shout out.

"You should all get along very well together. My three here adored our little Harry, who sadly passed away five months ago. They would all curl up on the sofa and fall asleep together", she continues.

'I don't think so', I say, as the middle cat moves towards me with a threatening hissing sound.

I immediately take two steps back.

I shall be keeping my distance from these three, that's for sure.

I'm still totally gutted that my family aren't here. I had really built up my hopes, only for them to be crumbled in seconds.

"Come and see the garden Penny. It is completely enclosed, and you can play out there to your hearts content", my new human tells me, as I follow her through two more doors.

'Now this is more like it', I say to myself, as I look around in amazement.

The garden is very well maintained, and high hedges surround the perimeter. Beautiful coloured flowers look to be popping out of large grey stones and an enormous green lawn looks very inviting.

"Off you go Penny. Have a good sniff around whilst I get your dinner ready and I will then show you where you will be sleeping tonight", she tells me.

I don't need telling twice and head off to investigate.

So many different smells to challenge my nose, although unfortunately a lot of them seem to be from the cats, you know, my new so-called brother and sisters.

'What a joke', I think to myself.

"Penny, your dinner is ready", I hear my new human call.

I dart into the house like a flash of lightning.

"Sit", she instructs me.

I do as she says, but cannot help the saliva dribbling from my mouth, as I sit patiently waiting for it to be served.

"Good girl", she tells me, as she places a food bowl onto the kitchen floor.

I have to say this is very delicious indeed and I make sure it is safely tucked away in my tummy in no time at all.

"My you were hungry, weren't you?" she tells me with a smile.

'Woof', I reply with a wag of my tail.

Suddenly, I am taken by surprise as my new siblings approach me. They are all hissing and sort of army crawling towards me.

"Now behave yourselves with your new sister", my human says, as she bends over to pick up my bowl.

I stand frozen to the spot, as Foxy jumps onto my humans back and takes a swipe at me with his right paw.

As quickly as I can, I turn my head, but I am not quick enough and suddenly I feel a sharp scratch to my right ear.

"Foxy. Get out of here now. What on earth has come over you?" she bellows at him.

"Penny are you ok?" she asks me, looking quite concerned.

I lower my head and watch as spots of blood drip down onto the kitchen floor.

"Oh, dear Penny, I am so sorry. Stay there a second whilst I get my first aid kit, so I can clean up your ear. I have never seen Foxy behave like this before. Hopefully, he will settle down and accept you soon", she tells me.

'I damn well hope so' I think to myself, in a very angry voice.

Who do these cats think they are?

I can see for sure, that I will need to have my wits about me at all times in this house.

I stand patiently whilst my human softly bathes my ear and applies some smelly cream onto my wound.

I let out a huge yawn.

"Penny, you sound like you are tired. Why don't you go out into the garden and do your toilet? Maybe you need an early night?" she asks me.

My yawn wasn't one of tiredness, it was one of stress. Why don't humans know this?

I saunter out into the garden and stoop down low for a wee. I feel as though I am being watched, but by whom?

Sitting on the wall behind me are Foxy, Lucy and Dora. They are glaring and hissing at me.

'Stand your ground Penny' I tell myself firmly, as I turn my back and ignore them.

I suddenly feel as though I am being followed. I stop and slowly turn around.

Foxy looks like he is ready to pounce again, so I turn and run as fast as I can back into the house with him closely on my heels.

I am running so fast, I nearly knock my human over, as I rush to hide under the kitchen table.

"What on earth is going on?" calls out my human, sounding very flustered.

Foxy has disappeared out of sight, but I don't trust him not to have another pop at me.

"Oh Penny. Hold on a minute. Stay here whilst I shut them in a different room for now. I am not having them terrorise you like this. It just isn't fair. Maybe I will just have to keep you all separated for the time being", I hear her say.

'*Now that sounds like a great plan to me*', *I say to myself, finally feeling relieved.*

Within five minutes she is back.

"Come on. It is safe to come out now. Look Penny, here is a new bed I bought ready for you. It looks lovely and cosy, don't you think? Do you like it?" she asks, as I army crawl my way out from underneath the table, looking left and to the right to check the coast is clear.

I must say it does look rather nice and comfy. It smells new too.

I jump onto my new bed and move around until I get into the right position.

'*Very nice*', *I say to myself.*

"Oh, and by the way, I bought you a little something else too", she smiles, as she walks away.

I lie intrigued, as I hear a plastic bag rustle.

I cannot believe what she is holding out to me. In her hands is a fluffy brown Teddy!

'How awesome is this?' I say to myself, as she gently places Teddy next to me.

I wrap my paws around him and place my head on his soft and squidgy tummy.

'Sweet dreams my friend', I tell him, as I let out a huge sigh of contentment.

Chapter 16

* * *

"Good morning Penny. Now what a good girl you were last night. Would you like to go out to the toilet?" my new human asks me.

I notice she is wearing what look to be pyjamas. They have pictures of cats all over them.

'How bizarre', I think, as I slowly get up and wag my tail at her.

"Right. Go on, off you go", she tells me.

I pick up Teddy and make my way out into the garden. I look to the left and then to the right to check the coast is clear. I sigh with relief when those horrible cats are nowhere to be seen.

'Phew', I say, as I start to relax.

I gently put Teddy down and do my business.

'Come on Teddy. Let's play', I tell him, as I trot around the garden throwing him into the air and then catching him.

I am so happy to have a Teddy back in my life.

"Penny. Your breakfast is ready", calls my human.

Teddy and I rush back to the kitchen as quickly as we possibly can.

'I must say the food here is rather good. I have never had rice before, but it seems to go down very well mixed with lots of chicken', I think to myself, as I continue to make sure there isn't a single grain left in my bowl.

"Now if you go back outside Penny, I will close the door and feed your brother and sisters. Is that ok?" she asks me.

I pick up Teddy and we make our way out into the garden once again. The glorious early morning sunshine feels very therapeutic all over my body.

I heard them say yesterday, it was early in the month of March, but to be honest I don't really know what that means.

'Meow', I suddenly hear.

'Oh no', I think to myself, as I slowly turn around to see Foxy glaring at me.

I thought my human was going to keep us all separated.

I quickly rush to pick up Teddy and dart towards the kitchen door, but it is firmly closed.

'How on earth did he get out?' I ask myself.

Michelle Holland

I suddenly hear a plop to my right, and I look around to see Lucy staring at me too. I cannot believe Dora is climbing out through a tiny kitchen window.

'Oh no', I think to myself, as I start to run as fast as I can to the other end of the garden.

'Meow, meow, meow. Hiss, hiss, hiss', is all I can hear.

I turn around to see all three are getting closer and closer. I dart around towards the back of the bushes, knocking heads off the poor flowers as I go with Teddy's dangling legs.

'They are not going to give in', I think to myself, as the three of them make their way towards me.

I drop Teddy and lie down low showing them my white teeth.

I growl, then bark as I lunge fiercely towards them.

Very sensibly Dora and Lucy move out of the way, but not Foxy, he is standing his ground and looking as though he is about to pounce again at any moment soon.

"What on earth is going on? How did you three get out here?" *my human is shouting, as I turn to see her rushing out of the kitchen door.*

I know I shouldn't have taken my eye off the ball and before I know it Foxy is flying in the air towards me hissing wildly.

I turn as fast as I can and run in the opposite direction. I skid around the corner at the back of the garden and my legs tumble beneath me. Before I know it, I've landed face first in a prickly rose bush.

"Penny. Are you ok?" I can hear my human shouting.

I stagger to my feet and realise I cannot open my right eye. It feels as though something is piercing it.

"Are you ok?" my human is asking me.

Using my good eye, I try hard to focus on where she is, and slowly make my way towards her.

"Oh Penny. What have you done poor love? Come here and let me have a look", she says in a very worried voice.

"Oh blimey", she says, as she takes a closer look.

"You have a large thorn sticking out from the top of your eyebrow down towards your eye lid. I just hope and pray it hasn't gone through to your eyeball. Come on Penny, I need to get you to the vets urgently", she tells me.

It feels very strange walking with one eye closed, but thankfully I manage to spot Teddy and pick him up.

"You are such a brave girl", my human is telling me, as she puts on my harness.

I blink constantly, as I feel tear drops rolling down my face.

"You want to bring Teddy too? Come on then let's go", she continues, as she walks slowly to the front door.

Back into the metal thing I get with Teddy by my side and off we go.

Chapter 17

* * *

It isn't long before we come to a standstill, and my human lets me out through the side door. We walk towards a very large white looking building.

'Oh no, there's that funny smell again. I wish Teddy had come in with me', I say to myself.

"Good morning Mrs Andrews. Please wait over there and Mr Thompson will see you shortly", says a lady sitting behind a desk pointing one claw towards a row of chairs.

"Penny Andrews please", a deep gruff voice calls out.

I follow my human and soon find myself inside a white-washed room with one of those familiar looking tables standing in the centre.

Unfortunately for me, I have seen these too many times in my very short life.

Michelle Holland

"Let's have a closer look at you Penny", says the gruff talking man.

"I feel terrible. It was my cat's fault this happened. I only brought Penny home yesterday and all they keep doing is constantly terrorising her. They were never like this with my Harry", replies my human.

"If I remember rightly, your Harry was a small and very low energy dog. Penny looks to me as if she is a pure-bred collie, with very high energy levels. Unfortunately, adding a new member to your household with such different energy levels, sometimes does not work out", he says, in quite a sad sounding voice.

"I am going to lift Penny onto the table and I want you to hold her head as still as you can", he continues, as he scoops me up as though I am as light as a feather.

I stand patiently whilst he looks closely at my eye.

"She has quite a large thorn piercing her eyebrow and it looks to be very close to her eyelid too. I will need to numb the area before I can check inside her eye", he says.

An unexpected sharp prick just above my right eye makes me jump and squeal.

"I am sorry Penny, I should have told you what I was about to do", he says apologetically.

"Now please hold her very still again", he informs my human.

I feel my eyelid being opened and I try to stay as still as I can.

"Penny is very lucky. The thorn has lightly scratched her eye, but thankfully hasn't pierced directly into it. She may need a couple of stitches once I have removed the thorn. She is a very lucky girl, as she could have lost her eye.", he tells us.

"Oh dear, this is all my fault", gasps my human in despair.

"Please hold her still, whilst I pull out that thorn", he instructs my human.

I feel something moving inside, a very weird sensation, but I don't feel any pain at all.

"Got it. Just look at the size of that, it is huge", he exclaims.

I suddenly feel some sort of fluid filling my bad eye and I am absolutely horrified to see droplets of blood drip down onto my human's hand.

"Right let's get this cleaned up and get a couple of stiches in", he says in a very matter of fact voice.

"Oh Penny, I am so sorry", whimpers my human.

"Penny will be fine. I shall give you some eye wash to use daily, and she will need to wear a collar to stop her from scratching her wound. As you well know, when it starts to heal, it will become very itchy", he replies, as he starts to clean up my face.

I then feel another weird sensation, as if something is pushing and pulling at the top of my eyebrow, but thankfully I still can't feel any pain.

"Good girl Penny. All done, I must say you were a very brave girl. Would you like a biscuit?", he asks.

'When do I ever refuse a biscuit?' I say to myself, instantly feeling much happier.

'This is yummy' I think, as he very kindly offers me a second one.

He lifts me down back onto the floor and the next thing I know I have a plastic lampshade stuck on my head once again.

'Charming', I say to myself, feeling very unhappy.

"If you wait out in reception, I will get her eye wash prescribed and ready. I would like to see her back here in one week's time", he tells us.

"Thank you very much Mr Thompson", replies my human.

It doesn't take long before we are back in the metal thing. I cannot tell you how relieved and pleased I am to see Teddy.

"Penny. I am really truly sorry, but I've had to make one of the hardest decisions I have ever had to make in the whole of my life. I have no choice but to return you to the rescue centre. It is breaking my heart, but I cannot put you at any more risk. It is obvious the cats haven't accepted you and I will promise you now, it is through no fault of your own. I am so sorry", she babbles.

'What does she mean? I don't want to go back to prison', I cry out, as I pull Teddy closer to me.

I honestly cannot believe it and feel truly gutted when she pulls up outside the familiar prison gates.

I watch with sadness as she disappears inside the building. It isn't long before she returns.

I gasp and start to feel anxious as the horrible carer who growls and shows her teeth at me is standing by her side.

The side door opens, my human unclips me and hands my lead over to the horrible carer.

"Please keep her harness, as it is so much nicer for her to walk in", pleads my human.

"Mrs Andrews, you might as well take that with you. We have no use for it here", growls my horrible carer.

"Can I come with you, so I can see her get settled in?" my human asks.

"No", she replies, in a very harsh tone.

'I want my Teddy', I say to myself, feeling panicky.

"Here is the eye wash and her Teddy. Penny seems very fond of him", says my human.

"You might as well keep that bear. We have enough crap in here already", she replies growling.

I can feel my eyes filling up with tears.

'I want my Teddy', I cry out.

Suddenly, I feel as if I am being choked, as my horrible carer drags me away from my human.

I glance back. She is holding her hands up to her face and I can see her shoulders moving up and down.

"Come on hurry up", my carer growls, as she pulls me roughly up the concrete steps.

I am finding it very hard to keep up, as my lampshade keeps catching, but she doesn't seem to care, and just keeps pulling me.

I try to stop to catch my breath, as I see the second set of concrete steps ahead, but no, she just continues to drag me.

I grimace and try to pull backwards, as I see the prison cells ahead with the familiar iron bars.

'I don't want to go back to prison', I scream out.

My horrible carer opens the prison door and forces me inside by kicking her boot up my backside. She then leans over to remove the lead from my collar.

I immediately decide I have had enough of this bully and take two steps backwards. I crouch down low and show my teeth, whilst growling at her in a very low tone.

"The feeling is mutual. You, horrible waste of space dog", she growls back at me, before locking the door and disappearing out of sight.

I can feel my pulse racing ten to the dozen.

'I have never behaved like that in the whole of my life', I think to myself, as I look around the cold and dismal cell.

All I can see is a dirty old towel and a bowl of water, no toys, no bed, nothing.

I walk over to the grubby towel and lay down, but my lampshade is making it hard for me to get comfy.

I feel mentally exhausted, confused, and lonely.

At this present moment I don't think I ever want to wake up.

Chapter 18

* * *

"Hi Penny, and how are you on this sunny Monday morning?" I hear Claire's cheerful voice asking me.

I am so pleased to see Claire, as I've been having some horrible flash backs in my dreams. I can feel dry, and crusty tears sitting under my eyes.

I immediately jump up and rush to greet Claire with my tail wagging as fast as it can possibly go.

"What a lovely welcome Penny. Thank you", she smiles at me.

I rush to pick up Teddy and drop him by the metal bars.

"Hey, bear with me. I've just got to serve up everyone's breakfast first and then I promise, we will go for a lovely walk. Would you like that? I shall be keeping a very close eye on you this morning, don't you worry", she tells me with a smile.

'Woof', I reply with another wag of my tail.

I wait eagerly for my food to arrive.

I so wish they would serve me some tasty food like the cat lady did.

Barking and whining instantly fills the air, as the old metal food trolley makes its way to every cell.

I sit patiently as Claire fills up my food bowl.

"I have given you a little extra as a treat, but promise me you won't tell anyone", she says with a grin.

I tuck into my breakfast and as usual Teddy isn't hungry.

'I wonder when Claire is coming back', I think to myself, as I pace up and down my cell.

Different size humans continue to walk past my cell, but for some reason they don't seem to be taking any notice of me.

"Here I am Penny. Come on, let's go for a walk and get some fresh air", Claire tells me.

I jump around in excitement as Claire unlocks my door. She clips a lead onto my collar and I just have enough time to pick up Teddy.

"I see your bear is coming for a walk with us too", she smiles.

Down the steps we go, around the corner, down some more and once again we arrive at my favourite patch of grass.

I do my business and turn to follow Claire.

I pick up Teddy and throw him high into the air. I watch as his little legs come dangling towards me and I gently catch him before he hits the ground.

I enjoy my leisurely walk with Claire, although she seems to be on another planet and constantly keeps checking her phone.

I wonder what on earth she is up to.

"We are going to have a longer walk than usual Penny, as I don't want to take you back inside until after nine-thirty", she tells me.

'Why not? What is going on?' I think to myself.

Claire plays with me, I sniff, then rest. We continue to do this for quite a while.

"Right Penny. The coast is clear, so we can make our way back now", she informs me.

I do as she asks, and we slowly make our way back to my cell.

I drop Teddy on our bed, as he looks to be totally exhausted.

"Have a little rest and I will be back shortly", she tells me, before disappearing out of sight.

I lay down next to Teddy, but suddenly a tall looking man with a very long beard is standing and staring at me through the metal bars.

I hate people staring at me. I have had months of this intrusion into my personal space, and I am not putting up with it anymore.

I jump into action and crouch down low. I show him my teeth whilst growling fiercely and he soon moves on.

'Ha ha', I laugh to myself, that didn't take him long to scurry away.

I suddenly stop and put my nose high into the air.

I can smell a very familiar scent, but where is it coming from?

"How is my Penny Pops this morning?" I hear Jo's soft voice asking me.

I cannot believe it, Jo is here. I am feeling elated.

My bum is wriggling totally out of control as I rush towards the metal bars to kiss her. My wet slobbery tongue manages to squeeze through the bars to lick her on her cheek.

"Now that is what I call a proper welcome", she grins back at me, as Claire appears at her side.

Chapter 19

✱ ✱ ✱

"Hey baby girl. How do you fancy coming home with me today?" smiles Jo.

For a moment, I cannot believe what Jo has just said. Does she really mean it, or maybe I just heard wrong? Am I dreaming? Do I need to pinch myself? I have so many different thoughts racing through my head at one hundred miles per hour.

I watch closely as Claire unlocks my door and Jo walks towards me.

I lunge into her wide-open arms and that warm and fuzzy feeling instantly returns throughout every part of my body.

"Could you pass me that harness please Claire? Oh, and Penny's new collar", Jo asks her.

'I have a new collar?' I say to myself, finding it very hard to contain my excitement.

I stand patiently whilst Jo fiddles with a few straps on this comfy feeling harness, and I can't help but lick her face as she leans over towards me.

The warm smile she gives me fills my heart with joy.

"There we go, now just look at you Penny Pops. Red is the perfect colour, for my perfect girl", she grins.

I have never felt so happy, in fact I am feeling very emotional with all this kindness and love I am being shown.

"Now let's put on your new red collar to match", continues Jo.

I cannot tell you how relieved I am when Jo takes off the heavy metal chain, I have had to carry around my neck for all this time.

I feel so much lighter already.

I can feel Jo's soft hands putting this material feeling collar around my neck.

'Wow, this feels so much better. It is so light. How lucky am I?' I grin to myself.

"You look gorgeous Penny", smiles Claire, with what looks to be tears running down her face.

'Why is Claire crying when I am feeling so happy?' I think to myself, feeling slightly confused.

At this precise moment I have that warm and fuzzy feeling again as I feel Jo's soft hand stroking my chest.

Michelle Holland

"Come on. Let's get you out of here Penny Pops, before nasty old Sharon makes an appearance. Claire could you bring her Teddy bear please?" asks Jo.

'My Teddy is coming too? I cannot believe this. Am I dreaming? Is this really happening?' I cry out loudly.

I stand patiently, as Jo clips a new red lead onto the front of my harness and clips the other end onto something on my back.

'How strange, I have never seen a harness like this before', I think to myself.

"Right my Penny Pops, this is where your new life begins and I can assure you now I will always be here to protect and look out for you", says Jo, as I stop to mark my favourite patch of grass before walking towards a row of metal things on wheels.

'I am surprised to feel no pressure at all on my neck. I am not used to walking this pain free', I smile to myself.

I jump backwards as a light suddenly flashes on the back of one of the metal things and makes a beeping sound.

"Penny Pops. I want you to meet Flicker, my chunky monkey", Jo grins.

Feeling slightly confused, I look all around me, but I cannot see any chunky monkeys anywhere.

"Is she going on the back seat of your car or in the boot?" I hear Claire ask.

"I will put Penny on the back seat, as Jacob normally goes in the boot", replies Jo.

It has just dawned on me after all this time that these metal things on wheels are in fact called cars.

I wonder why no-one ever told me this.

"Right Penny Pops, in you jump", grins Jo, as she opens the back door as wide as it will go.

I jump in as fast as I can. Jo attaches another clip onto the back of my harness and Claire leans over to put Teddy on the seat next to me.

'I cannot wait for our adventure to begin', I say to myself, as I put my nose high into the air.

There are so many different smells in here.

"Look at this they made me sign", I hear Jo telling Claire, as she puts a sheet of paper in front of her face.

"No way. You have got to be kidding me, right?" asks Claire, with a very startled look across her face.

"I am serious. I have also had to sign to say that me taking on Penny Pops, is completely against their wishes. It also states that Penny Pops must be muzzled at all times in public places", continues Jo.

'I wonder what a muzzle is?' I think to myself.

Michelle Holland

"What a bloody load of nonsense. If they had done their job properly in the first place and given her the exercise, training and mental stimulation she required, she wouldn't be in the state she is today. It is completely their fault and they will just not admit it. I am livid. Jo when you have gone, I am going to waltz into reception and tell them all to get stuffed. I will no longer be volunteering for them from this moment on", replies Claire, in a very angry voice.

"Good on you Claire", replies Jo, as she starts to wrap her arms around her.

"I am going to miss Penny", says Claire, as I see tears start to run down her face once again.

"You can visit Penny Pops anytime you want to, that goes without saying. Thank you also for looking out for her and for all the help and support you have given us both", says Jo, as she hands Claire a tissue.

"You make sure you take care Penny", says Claire, as she leans towards me to plant a single kiss onto the top of my head.

"I will text you later Claire", says Jo, before sitting on a seat which is directly in front of me.

"Right Penny Pops. Are you ready to go and meet Jacob, Daisy, Honey and Becky?" asks Jo.

'Woof', I reply, as the car starts to move.

I lean over as far as I can and just about manage to kiss the back of Jo's neck.

She turns to smile at me. That fuzzy and warm feeling shoots through the whole of my body once again.

Chapter 20

✶ ✶ ✶

"Not long now Penny Pops, we are nearly there. It is time to meet Jacob, Daisy, Honey and Becky", Jo tells me, as the car comes to a standstill.

I cannot believe the stunning countryside which surrounds us.

How awesome is this? Freedom at last', I think to myself feeling very, very happy.

"Out you get baby, time for us to go for a nice walk", she says, with a huge smile across her face, as she opens the door and unclips my seatbelt.

I quickly turn to pick up Teddy.

"Why not leave your bear here for now, as look what I have brought you to play with?" she grins, as she reaches into the front of the car and hands me a squeaky ball.

How lucky am I?

Inside A Dog's Mind

I proudly carry my ball as we walk over the beautiful South Downs. Occasionally, I stop to sniff and wee. There are so many new smells for me to investigate.

I love my new harness and lead. I don't have anything strangling my throat anymore and it makes everything feel so much more enjoyable.

"Come on, through this gate", Jo tells me.

I look around in glee at the amazing green paddock that lies ahead of me. It looks to have high fencing all the way around, and in the distance, I can see another human who looks to have three dogs on leads.

As we get closer to them, Jo suddenly calls out, "Becky, let's just walk about twelve feet apart from you for now".

The three dogs wag their tails and bark when they hear Jo's voice.

'This must be Jacob, Daisy, Honey and Becky', I suddenly think to myself.

"Penny, I need you to be on your best behaviour as Becky isn't as confident as me. Do you understand baby?" she asks me.

I look at Jacob who I must say is very handsome. He looks like a collie too, but he has shorter hair than me. He is black with a few white markings. Daisy looks like a big teddy bear and I would say she is about the same size as me. I can't wait to give her a cuddle, she looks very cute. Honey is the smallest, she's a sort of light brown little terrier type. Becky looks smaller than Jo and has jet black hair to match Jacob.

We continue to walk twelve feet apart. I glance over to see Jacob, Daisy and Honey are all busy sniffing.

"Oh Jo, she is more stunning in real life than on those photo's you showed me", calls out Becky.

"I know", grins Jo.

"Is it a good sign that they aren't taking any notice of each other Jo?" she calls back.

"Yes, it is a very good sign Becky. Let's keep reducing the space between us slowly and if they all stay relaxed and calm, we can let them off so they can greet each other properly", Jo replies.

"Can Penny be let off?" asks Becky sounding very surprised.

"Did you remember to bring the spare lunge line in your rucksack?" Jo replies.

"Of course, I did", laughs Becky.

I love the sound of humans laughing, although it has been a very rare occurrence in my short life.

"Becky. Could you get the spare lunge line out, and drop it onto the floor please? If you can then put Daisy and Honey's on too and just keep walking, that would be great. I will give you a signal when I feel it is the right time to let all three of them go", calls Jo. "Remember Becky, no eye contact with Penny. Ignore her and let her sniff, but do not go to touch her, however tempted you are. She is very insecure with people she doesn't know, continues Jo.

"Yes boss", calls back Becky.

I follow Jo across to where the lunge line lies on the ground and I feel her attach it onto the back of my harness before unclipping my lead.

"Ready when you are", Jo calls out.

'I am not sure what I need to be ready for, but I will give it my best shot', I think to myself.

Chapter 21

✷ ✷ ✷

I LOOK UP TO SEE Jacob, Daisy and Honey all running towards me at a tremendous speed. Cheeky Jacob comes to a halt and is naughtily sniffing my rear end, so I lift my tail higher to make it easier for him. Daisy is squealing with excitement and dancing around whilst play bowing at me. Honey is politely waiting for her turn to check me out too.

'I don't really know how to play with other dogs. Maybe she can teach me?' I say to myself.

Daisy turns her rear end around to me and I drop my ball, as I move forward to take a sniff.

I like the smell of her, and she is also very pretty.

I turn around to pick up my ball, but it isn't there. Where has it gone?

Can you believe Jacob has pinched it and he is standing with it firmly in his mouth whilst looking over at me?

Inside A Dog's Mind

"Aw Penny Pops, has Jacob pinched your ball?" laughs Jo. "Don't worry, trust me he'll soon get bored and drop it".

I turn to head off after Jacob, but I feel a tug on the back of my harness. I think Jo still has hold of the end of the lunge line which is attached to my back.

'Jo is so clever', I say to myself, as I watch Jacob drop my ball.

How on earth does she talk dog? I haven't got a clue, but I am very impressed.

"Drop Daisy's lunge line and I'll drop Penny's Becky. They can't escape from this secure field, so let's give them a chance to have a run around", calls out Jo.

Daisy runs straight towards me at full speed. I drop my ball in panic and start to run in the opposite direction.

I can hear Jo laughing.

I steer myself to the left and to the right. I know she's chasing me, but I am confident she won't catch me, as I have a tremendous amount of speed and turn of foot.

Daisy tries to round me up, but I am way too quick for her and she cannot keep up.

'Where has she gone?' I think to myself.

I look around to see where she is, and I smile as I see her laid flat out on the grass panting hard. I must have worn her out. It was great fun though.

"Penny come and have a drink of water", Jo is telling me.

I turn on a sixpence and race over to her as fast as I can.

"Wow, I cannot believe the speed Penny has Jo. No-one would know she has a metal pin in her hind leg", says Becky.

"I know Becky. She has probably never had this much freedom in her life. How awesome was that to see her running free and having such fun? Truly priceless and worth every single moment of the stress we've been through over the last couple of days", replies Jo.

"I totally agree", smiles Becky.

I am so thirsty, but Daisy is hogging the water bowl. I decide to be brave and take two steps forward and lean my mouth towards the water. I stick my tongue into the bowl next to Daisy's and I am so happy to see she doesn't mind me sharing her water.

'How cool is this? I hope me and her can be friends', I think to myself feeling happy.

"Aw that is so sweet", coos Becky. "Good girl for sharing Daisy".

"Come on. I think it's time to get you lot home. Have we got everything?" asks Jo.

"Where is Penny's new ball?" replies Becky.

"Good question, I'll go and have a look. No, hang on, watch this Becky. Penny Pops go and find your ball", Jo commands me.

Off I go in search of my ball. I sniff, I turn until I'm confident I am on the scent of my ball.

'To the left', I tell myself.

I can smell my ball isn't too far away.

'There you are', I call out, as I pounce on the top of my ball, grab hold of it and run back to Jo.

"Wow Jo. How awesome was that?" Becky says, sounding very impressed.

"I told you she was intelligent and a very fast learner, didn't I?" beams Jo, as she picks up my ball and puts it safely away in her pocket.

"Clever girl Penny Pops", she tells me, as she clips my lead onto my harness before rolling up the lunge line.

'I cannot tell you how happy I am feeling at this present moment. Probably the happiest I have ever felt in my life', I think to myself.

Chapter 22

* * *

"There you go Penny Pops, in you get", Jo is telling me, as she opens the back door of the car.

To be honest I am slightly confused as to why Becky is putting Jacob, Daisy and Honey into a different car.

"See you at home", says Jo, as she waves to Becky.

Teddy is still where we left him on the back seat. I am thrilled to see he seems happy and content too.

It isn't long before the car stops outside a very nice-looking house. I watch with interest as another car pulls up right next to us and out jump Becky, Jacob, Daisy and Honey.

I am relieved when Jo picks up Teddy, as I jump out of the car. We follow Becky, Jacob, Daisy and Honey through a gate and then inside a door into a sort of utility room. Jo leaves my harness on but unclips my lead.

"Go and have a look around Penny Pops", urges Jo, as I watch Jacob, Daisy and Honey all disappear through another open door.

I am feeling a little apprehensive and nervous. I don't really want to leave Jo's side.

"Come on silly. Go on, I'll come with you then", laughs Jo.

Slowly, I follow her into a lovely big hallway. From here I can see what looks like a bedroom, a lounge with two comfy dog beds, a large kitchen and I am amazed when I look behind me to see another huge dog bed and the biggest box of toys I have ever seen.

'Wow, oh wow', I think to myself, as I spot the numerous teddy bears and cannot believe how many balls there are too.

"Hey Penny Pops. You can play with any of Jacob, Daisy and Honey's toys. We believe caring is sharing", smiles Jo.

"Come on, let me show you around", she continues.

I stick to Jo like glue. I don't want to leave her side. She always makes me feel safe.

"Right Penny Pops", she says, as she walks up the stairs.

'I love the feeling of the relaxing and calm energy inside this house', I think to myself.

"This is where you will be sleeping for now. That is mine and Becky's bed there. Your bed is right next to my side by the radiator and Jacob, Daisy and Honey sleep on their beds next to Becky", she tells me.

'I like this layout very much. It means I can keep an eye on Jo and make sure she is always safe. How cool is this?' I smile to myself

"This is the bathroom, which reminds me, I need to spend a penny so to speak", she continues.

'Now I am confused. Why does she want to spend me?' I think with slight panic.

"Stay here for a second, I will be back in a moment", she tells me, as she closes the door to the bathroom.

'I can't see her. Jo, Jo, are you ok?' I cry out, and with all the force I can gather, I throw myself at the door.

"Penny Pops. What is the matter, are you OK?" asks a very shocked Jo, who for some reason is sitting on a strange object with her trousers pulled down to her ankles.

"Hey, don't worry, I am only going to the toilet", she tells me, as she strokes me softly under my chin.

"Oh dear. It looks like you have lots of horrible and matted knots around your throat Penny Pops. I'll need to cut them out. Let me finish off what I am doing, and then I'll pop and find my scissors", she says, as she suddenly stands up, and fixes her trousers back into the right place.

I watch intrigued. I am taken aback as I hear water coming from out of the object she was sitting on. I move closer to investigate and I am shocked to see a giant water bowl. I have never seen one so big.

"Hold on, let me put the toilet seat down", Jo tells me.

I cannot believe it. The water bowl now has a lid on it. I have never seen anything like this in the whole of my life.

Jo is now standing next to another object and I can hear water once again. I jump up to investigate and I am very surprised to see lots of water running out of a metal object.

"I bet you have never seen anything like this before, have you baby?" Jo asks me.

"Look. It is nice fresh water", she tells me, as she makes a cup shape with her hands, fills it with water and offers it to me.

I gently lap the fresh cold water from her hands, as I continue to stand on my hind legs. I have to say it tastes rather good.

"You want some more?" Jo asks me, as she fills up her hands with water once again.

I lean forward and lap it up in no time. The metal thing is still running so I lean forward as far as I can and drink the water straight from the running tap.

Michelle Holland

"What a clever girl. I cannot believe you are drinking water straight from the tap", beams Jo.

She dries her hands on a towel and I follow her closely into another room.

Chapter 23

* * *

"This is my office where I work from every day. I sometimes need to go out on appointments, but I am never out for long and Becky also has an office downstairs, so you will be never be left on your own. What do you think to this Penny Pops? It means you can stay with me whilst I am working, that is if you want to of course" she continues.

'Am I hearing right? Will I really be spending every day with Jo?' I ask myself, quite not believing what she just said.

"Right. Let me find those scissors", says Jo, as she rummages inside her desk drawer.

"Becky you won't believe how many knots Penny Pops has around her throat and ears. They must be so uncomfortable. I'm just going to make a start on cutting them out", she shouts out.

"Ok. I will just put the kettle on and get their dinner ready then", Becky calls back.

Jo very slowly sits down next to me.

"Now I need you to stay still and trust me. Here have a treat Penny Pops", she smiles, as she opens her little magic tin. I watch as she opens and closes a pair of scissors for me to see.

I trust Jo and I know she isn't going to hurt me. I stand as still as I possibly can. The sound of the scissors opening then closing, goes on for quite a while.

"What a very brave girl you are", Jo tells me, as I open my eyes. I am very surprised to see a very large pile of what looks to be my hair sitting on the floor beside her.

"Let me make sure you haven't got any more of those nasty knots anywhere", she says, as she runs one hand gently under my tummy.

This feels rather ticklish. I can't stop my right hind leg, as it starts to rise into the air.

"I cannot believe how matted you are between your back legs too. This must have felt so uncomfortable. I bet you have never been groomed before either, have you?", she continues whilst tutting.

'I have never heard anyone mention the word groomed, so I don't really know what that means', I think to myself, feeling rather puzzled.

"You need to trust me even more now. I am going to lay on my back and put my head under your belly. I will get the worst off for now and I can get rid of the rest during this week", she tells me, in a very calm voice.

I close my eyes and once again try to stay as still as I can. I can hear the scissors busily working away, and it isn't too long before Jo stops, and offers me a treat.

"What a good girl you are. I cannot believe the state you're in under there. Your coat has been totally neglected", Jo tuts, as I look at the growing pile of my hair by her side.

"Their dinner is ready", calls Becky.

'Now this is more like it', I say to myself', as I follow Jo back down the stairs.

"I have given them all wet kibble, chopped up chicken with carrots and a few frozen peas. I have added a bit of that food you brought back with you from the rescue centre, but to be honest it smells really crappy", says Becky, as she screws up her nose.

'I am glad to hear that at last someone else agrees with how awful the food was that I was forced to eat daily', I mumble to myself.

"Right Becky, if you put Jacob's bowl in the hallway, I'll feed the three girls here in the kitchen", says Jo.

I watch closely as Becky walks past me with a bowl of something that smells truly delicious.

"Daisy sit", commands Jo, as she immediately obliges.

I watch as Jo gently puts a food bowl onto a wooden table looking thing which seems to have two large holes in it.

"Honey sit", she continues, as she places another bowl onto the floor.

'Hurry up Jo', I cry out.

My dribble has started to drool uncontrollably from my mouth and no matter how hard I try I cannot control it.

"Penny Pops sit", asks Jo.

I do as she asks and as soon as the bowl is on the floor, I gobble it all down in seconds without even stopping to take a breath.

"Slowly Penny", I can hear Jo say, but this is the tastiest meal I have had in the whole of my life and I don't want any of the others pinching it.

"OMG, I have never seen a dog eat like that before. She ate it all so fast, she is probably going to be sick", says Becky, who I notice has her hands covering her face.

"Me neither Becky. We don't know how long she was a stray for in Ireland and maybe she has never tasted food this good before? Don't worry, I know how to resolve this. You can buy slow feeding bowls to stop dogs from bolting their food. They have circle like puzzles inside them and it also helps with their digestion. If I order one tonight, it should be here by tomorrow", replies Jo.

'I cannot believe that Jo can read my mind so quickly. How cool is she?' I think to myself.

Chapter 24

* * *

"Right come on guys, you probably all need to go out to the toilet now. Follow me", instructs Jo, as we all walk through another door and out into the fresh air.

I am surprised to see a lovely garden with high fences and a large green area of grass.

I follow Daisy and quickly turn to check Jo is close by. I trot up and down the bouncy grass trying to keep in a straight line. I notice some steps going up onto a lovely balcony, so off I go up the steps, then back down and begin my routine all over again. I can see that Jacob, Daisy and Honey are looking at me in a very odd way.

'I wonder why they don't behave like I do. They seem so chilled out' I say to myself.

"Why is Penny pacing like that?" I hear Becky ask.

"This is what she got used to doing all the time for the last three months, just pacing up and down a concrete kennel. This is all she has known. It is a habit which we can hopefully break with time", Jo replies.

"Poor love", replies Becky.

"Penny Pops. Look what I've got", I can hear Jo calling.

I immediately stop pacing and dash over to Jo. I am thrilled to see she has my ball.

"Come on let's play with your ball. It will be a lot more fun than pacing up and down the garden", she tells me.

'I think I can manage to play some ball', I reply, as I crouch down low waiting readily.

"Ready steady go", calls Jo, as the ball comes flying towards me.

'Got it. Easy peasy', I think to myself, as I run back to Jo.

"Penny Pops drop", Jo commands.

I do as she asks and drop the ball not far from her feet.

"Watch this Becky", she continues, with a big grin across her face.

"Penny Pops push", she tells me.

I stoop down low, get closer to my ball and with my nose I push it as hard as I can straight across to Jo.

I laugh to myself as I watch it roll in between Jo's legs.

Off I go to retrieve it, before Jo has even had time to turn around.

"I have never seen a dog push a ball before. She is so clever and so fast", I hear Becky say.

"I know she has the speed of lightning", replies Jo.

"I bet she would be awesome at flyball Jo. Maybe that's something I can do with her in the future, to help us bond. What do you think?" asks Becky.

"That sounds like a fabulous idea. It would be good for both of you", smiles Jo.

'I am a little bit confused. Why on earth would I want to go and watch a fly play ball? Seems a bit stupid to me', I say to myself.

"Right come on. Time to go inside and have some quiet time", says Jo.

I stay close to Jo and follow her into the lounge.

Jacob is laid on a bed and is glaring at me as I walk past him. He gives me a dirty look and curls his top lip up.

"Jacob, we will have none of that behaviour thank you", Jo tells him, in a very soft voice.

He looks directly at her and wags his half tail.

I wonder what happened to his tail.

Daisy is funny. She is laid flat out on her back on one of the sofas with her legs high up in the air.

Inside A Dog's Mind

Honey is curled up on Becky's lap, looking very snug indeed.

I watch as Jo sits next to Becky. I move as close as I can to Jo.

"You really are beautiful", Becky tells me.

She is staring at me and I feel very uncomfortable.

'Grrrrr', I warn her, as I jump into attack mode.

"Oh no you don't Penny Pops", says Jo, as she quickly grabs the back of my harness to stop me lunging at Becky.

Honey growls loudly at me, as Becky holds her back.

"That scared me a little bit Jo. Why did she want to go for me?" asks Becky sounding a little shaken.

Now I feel very bad. I am so used to behaving like this over the last few months, that I just can't help myself. I really need to try hard to learn how to control my outbursts of anger.

"Becky, you were staring at her for too long. I told you it makes her feel uncomfortable. Maybe it is the colour of your hair?" Jo replies, as I continue to sit by her side.

Jo is still holding onto my harness and Jacob continues to give me a dirty look. He doesn't look happy with me, neither does Honey, but Daisy hasn't moved an inch.

Michelle Holland

"We are going to have to be on our guard at all times Becky. We need to keep their energies as low as we possibly can, as I don't want anything kicking off. Don't forget, Honey goes off to her new forever home the day after tomorrow", says Jo.

"I am really going to miss my little gremlin", coos Becky, as she continues to kiss her.

"Me too Becky, this fostering lark is very hard. You cannot help getting so attached to them, but I know Honey will have all the love she needs. She will be spoilt and treated like the princess she is" replies Jo, with what look to be tears in her eyes.

'I have heard this word foster before. I hope Jo won't send me to live with someone else', I think, as I suddenly start to feel slightly panicky.

Chapter 25

✳ ✳ ✳

"Well I don't know about you Jo, but I feel completely shattered and could probably do with an early night", announces Becky.

"To be honest, it has been a long day for all of us and I feel tired too. Maybe we can watch a film in bed?" asks Jo.

I am not quite sure what watching a film means, but I am happy to give it a go.

"That sounds a great idea. Why don't you let the dogs out for a wee, whilst I finish off tidying up the kitchen?" says Becky.

"Come on guys, it is time for you to go to the toilet. Come on lazy bones", she tells Daisy, as she plants a kiss on her head.

Jacob is the first to dash out the door like a flash of lightning, followed by Honey, and then Daisy. Me and Jo follow closely behind them all.

Jacob is cocking his leg up at one of the bushes.

"Go on Penny Pops toilet", Jo tells me.

I begin to pace up and down again, but soon come to a complete stop when I smell a lovely scent floating towards my nose. I head towards where Daisy has just wee'd. It smells good and I cannot resist stooping down and weeing on top.

"Good toilet Penny Pops", Jo is saying, sounding very excited.

"Come on, in you all come. You can each have a biscuit before bed", she continues.

Now that sounds more like it, *I say, as I race to follow the gang inside.*

Jo asks us all to sit in the utility room and one by one, she rewards us with a very tasty cheese biscuit.

"Right bedtime", she says.

Immediately Jacob, Daisy and Honey head off up the stairs at a very fast pace.

"Hey you lot, steady now. You sound like a herd of elephants running up those stairs", she shouts out to them.

I closely follow Jo up the stairs, sticking to her like glue.

There is a lot of noise coming from the bedroom. I can hear human voices. Where did they come from?' I think to myself, feeling slightly confused.

Inside A Dog's Mind

I feel on edge as I slowly follow Jo into the bedroom. The only humans I can see are Jo and Becky, so where are the others hiding? I look up at Jo to ask her if she knows where they are.

"Becky. Can you turn the sound down on the television please?" she asks her.

I am confused, the voices are now whispering, but where are they hiding?

"I bet Penny Pops has never seen a television before Becky. Look, this is a TV baby. It isn't going to hurt you I promise", she tells me, as she points to this large flat square thing sitting on the top of a set of drawers.

I still don't really understand, but instantly feel better, now Jo has told me nothing is going to hurt me.

"On your bed Penny Pops", Jo tells me, as she points towards a comfy looking bed next to a radiator.

I do as she asks and walk over to the bed. It smells fresh and clean. I lie down and think to myself this is the comfiest bed I have ever slept on.

I keep a close eye on Jo, as she takes some clothes off and puts on what looks to be a pair of pyjamas. She then pulls back a white blanket over the top of her and suddenly disappears.

I immediately start to panic. I need to find Jo. Where has she gone?

"Hey what's the matter?" Jo asks, as she lifts her head up from underneath the blanket.

I cannot tell you how relieved I am to see that she is ok, and I wag my tail in happiness.

"Hey, it's ok. You are just feeling insecure aren't you", smiles Jo, as she sits up and gently strokes me.

"Penny Pops, go and lay back down and get some sleep", she tells me.

I do as she says but decide to keep one eye open and one ear up just to be on the safe side.

I must have nodded off. I open my eyes to see everything is completely dark and I desperately need to go to the toilet, so I paw at the duvet covering Jo.

She groans and rolls over.

'Maybe if I go downstairs and tap on the door like Mum used to tell us to do?' I think to myself.

I can hear Honey and Daisy snoring away. Jacob opens one eye as I walk past him to make my way downstairs.

I tap at the door with my front right paw, but no-one comes down to let me out. I really need to go for a poo. I continue to pace up and down, back and forth from the lounge I go. No matter how hard I try, I cannot hold on any longer and have no option but go to the toilet at the far end of the lounge, just like I used to do in my cell. I sneak back up the stairs and Jacob barks at me, as I try to sneak back onto my bed.

Jo instantly awakes and sits upright in bed.

"Are you ok Penny Pops?" she whispers to me. "Do you need the toilet?".

'A little bit late for that,' I say to myself, but wag my tail and immediately jump up.

"Come on then", Jo says, rubbing her eyes.

I follow Jo down the stairs, and she opens the back door. I rush out into the garden, have a quick wee and dash back inside to find her.

I immediately feel guilty, as I watch her clearing up my poo in the lounge. I stand and wait for her reaction.

Am I going to get told off?

"Hey baby girl, everyone has accidents. Please don't worry", she whispers to me.

I walk across to her slowly and ask for reassurance.

"As it is only three o'clock in the morning, rather than wake the others up, why don't we sleep down here for the rest of the night?" she asks me, with a smile.

'Oh yes', I shout out, as I wag my tail.

I follow her into the downstairs bedroom and watch her get into bed.

"Sweet dreams Penny", she tells me, as I settle down onto a bed on the floor.

I try to get back to sleep, but I am finding it very difficult, so I decide to get up and wander around to find Teddy.

Jo stirs and sits up in bed.

"Penny Pops come here. What is the matter?" she asks me, as I walk towards her.

"Aw bless your heart. Don't you look so cute holding your bear", she smiles.

I immediately wag my tail.

"Come on jump up on here and snuggle down with me, but don't tell Becky", she tells me.

I don't need telling twice and within seconds I am lying next to Jo, with Teddy safely by my side. My head is on a very comfortable pillow next to Jo's. I look into her eyes, and she smiles back. That warm and fuzzy feeling instantly flows through every single part of my body. At last, I feel happy and content, and eventually my tired eyes begin to close.

Chapter 26

* * *

My first week at Jo and Becky's has flown by very quickly indeed, the total opposite to when I lived in prison where the days had always seemed endless. Honey went off to her new home three days after I arrived, and Jo and Becky had both cried when she'd gone.

I am still not too sure around Becky, although she does seem to be keeping her distance from me which is making me feel slightly more comfortable. There was only one occasion when I nearly messed up. We were all getting our harnesses on in the utility room to go out for a walk when Becky appeared out of nowhere and made me jump. I couldn't help myself and instantly dived towards her continuously growling and barking. Jo had immediately grabbed hold of my harness and kept us completely apart until I had calmed down. As usual Jacob had given me an evil look, but Daisy didn't take any notice.

Michelle Holland

We have been somewhere different on our walks every day. The countryside where I live is so beautiful and there are so many smells to keep us all busy. I still pace up and down in the garden, but I am finally starting to relax and chill out, so I am not having the urge to do it quite as often. I've had two more accidents in the middle of the night, but Jo and Becky thankfully don't seem to be angry with me.

I also have a new food bowl and I've never seen anything like this before. It is made of plastic and has circular patterns inside. At first, I found it very frustrating, as it doesn't allow me to eat my food as fast as I am used to. I will certainly persevere with it though, as the food I am served here is the best I have ever tasted.

Thankfully, Teddy seems happy and contented too, although Jacob did pinch him one day and refused to let me have him back. I'd sat for ages waiting for him to drop Teddy, but he just held him tightly in his mouth and kept glaring at me. Eventually, Jo had popped her head around the corner and asked him if he'd wanted a biscuit. Thankfully he released Teddy straight away.

Daisy is very comical. One day she chased me around and around the lounge. I'd had to jump on the sofas and bounce down onto the bean bag as I attempted to escape from her. Cushions had flown

Inside A Dog's Mind

left right and centre scattering themselves all over the lounge, before I'd raced up the stairs to the safety of Jo and hid away under her desk.

    I did have a bit of a melt down on Thursday. There is another huge oblong bowl in the bathroom that normally stays empty. I'd watched closely as Jo had turned two taps on and suddenly the water started to fill up the bowl. There were lots of bubbles rising out of the bowl too. I couldn't believe it when Jo took off all her clothes, jumped into the bowl and completely disappeared. I'd panicked and immediately rushed over to save her. Her head was under the water and I couldn't see her for all those bubbles. I'd barked as loudly as I could whilst jumping up against the bowl trying to find her. I'd jumped back in surprise. I was a little shocked to see that when she eventually appeared from out of the bowl, loads of white bubbles were stuck onto the top of her head. In fact, it looked like she was wearing one of those plastic lampshades. I cannot tell you how relieved I was to see that she was ok. I'd decided to stay right next to the bowl leaning my head over the top so I could keep a close eye on her. It wasn't long before she'd climbed out and I'd watched in disbelief as the water and bubbles slowly vanished through a tiny hole at the bottom of the bowl.

Michelle Holland

How amazing is this?

On Friday, Jo told me we were going to meet someone very special on our walk. I'd wondered if she had managed to find my Mum. Jacob and Daisy had gone for a separate walk with Becky and as me and Jo made our way up the driveway, I couldn't believe it when I saw Claire standing at the top. I'd literally dragged Jo towards her, wagging my bum and tail in all directions, as I couldn't contain my excitement.

"Penny just look at you", grinned Claire, as she continued to make a big fuss of me.

The three of us had then gone on a lovely long walk across the stunning South Downs.

Chapter 27

✶ ✶ ✶

"Good girl Penny Pops", Jo is telling me, as she picks up my empty breakfast bowl, before proceeding to get Jacob's and Daisy's.

"Give me just an hour or so to catch up on some work and then we can all go out for a wonderful walk", she tells me.

I follow her up the stairs and sit under her desk, putting my head into her lap. She gently strokes me around my neck, but suddenly stops.

She immediately jumps off her office chair and calls me over to her and kneels at my side.

"What the flipping heck is this?" she is saying out loud, as she continues to feel all around my neck.

"Becky, Becky come here quickly", she calls out loudly.

I haven't a clue what is going on.

Michelle Holland

I hear footsteps rushing up the stairs and within seconds Becky appears with Jacob and Daisy by her side.

"What on earth is the matter?" asks Becky.

"Penny Pops has an enormous lump on the right side of her neck. It is the size of a satsuma. Becky it wasn't there yesterday I can assure you", replies Jo, sounding anxious.

"Do you think she will let me have a look?" replies Becky, as she takes two steps towards me.

I immediately growl at her and she backs off quickly.

"I'll take that as a no then. Jo you need to take her to the vets to get her checked out straight away. Why don't you get her ready and I will give them a call to see if they have any emergency appointments available", she continues, before disappearing.

"Ok thanks", says Jo.

"Come on baby, let's go and get your harness on", Jo says to me, as we head down the stairs.

"They can see you in ten minutes Jo. I hope she is going to be ok", calls Becky.

"Me too. I will take the mesh muzzle too just in case", says Jo, as she pops on my harness and we head off out the front door.

'I wonder where we are going?' I think to myself.

It isn't long before we enter this building which looks like a house.

As soon as we walk through the second door, that old familiar smell wafts up my nostrils and I start to panic. It reminds me of not so nice memories.

"Come on Penny Pops. We just need to get you checked out. I promise I will stay with you", Jo is telling me softly.

"Could you pop Penny onto the scales please?" asks a lady, who is sitting behind a desk.

'I haven't a clue what a scale thing is, but I hope it isn't going to hurt', I think to myself.

Jo holds out a tasty biscuit in front of my nose and slowly moves it away from me. I follow the treat and suddenly I am standing on a different kind of surface.

"Nineteen point one", Jo calls, out with a smile, as she hands me over another treat.

"You are such a clever girl Penny Pops. I love you", she tells me, whilst planting a kiss on the top of my head.

I love it when she kisses me. It always makes me feel warm and fuzzy.

"Penny please", calls out a different human voice.

"Come on this way", Jo tells me, as we head through another door.

It is a white room with one of those tables standing in the middle.

'Oh gripes', I groan to myself.

Jo keeps me facing her, as she continues to feed me tasty treats.

"Penny doesn't like anyone staring at her, she suffers with fear aggression. We are fostering her as she was going to be PTS and we have only had her a week. This morning I found a huge lump on her neck and it certainly wasn't there yesterday", Jo tells her.

"Ok, I'll need to have a feel of it so I can check it out properly. It may be safer to pop that muzzle on and I will slowly approach from the side", replies the lady.

"Penny Pops. I need you to trust me. I am just going to put this muzzle on. It won't be for long, I promise", Jo tells me, as she fits this mesh thing over my nose and fastens a clip behind my ears.

"Good girl, that's it. Now, please stay still", Jo asks me, as she holds my head round to the left.

I suddenly feel a strange hand moving around my neck.

"You are so brave my baby. I am so proud of you", says Jo, as she holds me close to her.

The hand suddenly stops. Jo unclips the mesh thing and gives me a treat, followed by a kiss.

Inside A Dog's Mind

"There is quite a mass sitting on her lymph nodes. I will need to take a biopsy to send off to the lab. Can you bring her over to our main surgery tomorrow morning? We can't do anything today because she has already eaten. Please starve her from midnight tonight and I will see you at eight thirty am. No water either from six am tomorrow morning too. It might be best if you could stay at the surgery whilst she has the procedure. She will probably need stitches and it would be a lot less stressful for her given what she has been through, if you are with her when she goes under and comes around from the anaesthetic. She is also under weight and could probably do with putting a couple of kilos on. Just increase her daily food allowance, but only on a gradual basis.", she continues.

"Of course, Penny is on a much more nutritious diet than she is used to, and I did think she was on the lean side, probably down to the stress she has gone through. I was going to ask you if I could stay with her whilst you put her under and be there for her when she wakes up. How long will it take for the results to come back from the lab?" Jo asks.

"Usually within seven days", replies the lady.

"Ok thank you. We will see you in the morning then", replies Jo with a smile.

"Let's go home baby girl", Jo tells me, much to my relief.

Chapter 28

✳ ✳ ✳

"I AM NOT GOING TO leave you Penny. I want you to be brave and I will be by your side when you wake up, I promise. We can then go home, you can get some rest and I can spoil you with some nice chicken to make up for missing your breakfast this morning", Jo tells me.

'My tummy is rumbling. I am so hungry', I say to myself, not sure what is going to happen to me. I have an idea it isn't going to be pleasurable, as I smelt that old familiar smell as soon as we walked in here.

"Good morning Jo and Penny. Please follow me", says the familiar lady from yesterday.

We follow her into this little room, and I am very relieved to see there isn't a table in here.

"I will give Penny her pre-med now and once she has fallen asleep, my colleague will pop in and take her down to theatre", she continues.

'I wonder what a theatre is. I am certainly not ready to have a sleep yet, as it still only the morning', I think to myself, feeling slightly confused.

"If you hold Penny like you did yesterday, I will pop the needle into her front left leg and then back away slowly. Is that ok?" she asks Jo.

"Of course, but please take very good care of her for me", Jo replies.

Jo has hold of my head and is looking straight into my eyes.

"Of course, we will", says the lady, as I feel a sharp prick in my front leg.

"Penny Pops, you are such a brave girl, do you know that?" she is telling me, as my legs start to feel wobbly.

I can't seem to focus on Jo, my eyes have gone blurry and feel so heavy. I try as hard as I can to keep them open, but I cannot and suddenly everything goes black.

I open my eyes and am so happy to see Jo's smiling face looking down at me.

"Hey, don't move yet baby. Please just take your time to wake up properly", she is telling me.

I can feel her hand gently caressing my chest and I feel warm and fuzzy.

I try to stand up, but my legs feel wobbly and I have a strange tingling sensation in my neck.

"Steady", Jo tells me, as she supports my body.

"Let me just pop your harness on and then when you feel ready, we can take a few steps", she tells me, in a very soft voice.

I look down at my front left leg to see a bald patch. Someone has shaved me, but why?

"That's it slowly, slowly,", coaxes Jo, as I take my first step forward.

I feel light-headed, as I try hard to get my balance and it isn't long before we are in the reception area.

'I just want to go home', I cry out.

"Now Jo, here are the antibiotics to stop any infection setting into her wound and it should also start to reduce the swelling. One in the morning and one in the evening for seven days. You also have some Metacam, nineteen mils daily, although Penny won't need any until tomorrow morning, as I have already given her some pain relief. She has five dissolvable stiches, so just keep a close eye on them, as she may be tempted to scratch that area with her back leg. We can't put a collar on her due to where her wound is. If you have any concerns at all, just call us straight away, day or night. I would just let her have gentle lead walks from tomorrow for a few days and try to keep her as calm as possible. We need to make sure she doesn't burst those stitches", says the familiar lady we saw earlier, who now looks to be dressed in a gown.

'What wound? What stitches? The only thing I can see different is a shaved patch on my front leg and that isn't bleeding. What on earth is she talking about?' I think to myself.

"Thank you", smiles Jo, as she takes hold of a bag from the lady.

"Don't worry, I will call you as soon as the results are in", she replies.

"Come on my Penny Pops, let's get you home", Jo tells me, as we slowly walk out to the car park.

I still feel woozy and wobbly as Jo opens the back door. I try to lift my weight off the ground to jump in, but I don't have any energy at all. Suddenly, Jo scoops me up into her arms and gently lifts me on to the back seat and clips on my seat belt.

"There you go. Good girl. Now, just you rest whilst I concentrate on getting us home safely", she tells me, before planting a kiss onto the top of my head.

I close my eyes as the car starts to move and feel totally exhausted.

Chapter 29

* * *

"Wakey, wakey sleep head. We are home", I hear Jo's voice telling me.

I try hard to get my bearings, as Jo tries to gently coax me out of the car. I still have no energy.

"Ok Penny Pops. Just hang on a second and I will lift you out", she says smiling down at me.

It isn't long before I feel myself being lifted into Jo's arms. She gently puts me down and I am happy to have my four paws safely on the driveway.

I look up to see Becky, Jacob and Daisy waiting for us at the front door, as we slowly make our way in. Daisy is whining and wagging her tail at the same time. I am happy she seems so pleased to see me. Jacob doesn't give me an evil look for once, he just puts his nose up high into the air and continues to sniff.

Inside A Dog's Mind

"Aw Penny, Jo told me how brave you have been", says Becky with a big smile, as we make our way through to the lounge.

"Could you get Penny some of that freshly chopped up chicken from the fridge please Becky", Jo asks her, as she gently takes off my harness.

Now she has mentioned the word chicken, my stomach immediately starts to gurgle away.

"There we go", says Jo, as she offers me very small pieces of chicken.

I can see Becky giving Jacob and Daisy some too.

"That is enough for now baby, you can have some more in about an hour's time. Now I must pop upstairs to send a few work emails, so I need you stay here and rest. Is that ok?" she tells me.

"I don't mind staying with her for a while, whilst you crack on with work?" offers Becky.

"That would be a great help, thank you. I'll pop and wash my hands first, so just call me if you need me", Jo says, as she gets up to move.

'No, I want you to stay with me, not Becky. I still don't feel well', I cry out, as I struggle to get up.

My legs feel wobbly, as I take a few steps.

"Hey Penny. Come here and lie down next to me", says Becky.

I turn my head, curl up my lip and growl.

"Jo this isn't going to work. Penny wants you", I hear her shout out.

Within seconds Jo is back by my side and I sigh with relief.

"Why don't I bring your laptop down here for you. You can sit on the sofa and work whilst keeping an eye on Penny", says Jo.

"Good idea. Could you also bring my diary and phone charger down please?" Jo replies.

I watch as Becky runs up the stairs with Jacob following closely behind. Within minutes she is back with a piece of equipment which I didn't know was called a laptop, as it normally sits on the top of her desk. As she makes her way towards Jo, I growl once again.

"Penny Pops come on, that's enough please", Jo says to me, as she takes the piece of equipment from Becky.

I lay down next to Jo's legs and put my head on her slippers. I cannot get comfy and continue to fidget around. Daisy is fast asleep on the other sofa laid on her back with her legs in the air as usual.

"Hey, poor baby, you can't you get comfy, can you?" Jo asks, as she puts her laptop down onto the nearby table.

'I love the way Jo can read my mind', I think to myself with a smile.

Inside A Dog's Mind

"Here we go", says Jo, as she gently lifts me up onto the sofa, next to where she had been sitting. Jo picks up her laptop and sits back down next to me. I shuffle my body closer to her until I am touching her legs and I instantly start to feel better. I listen to the tiny tapping noise she makes as she works away.

"Would you like a coffee?" asks Becky, as she suddenly appears at the doorway.

"Yes please", Jo calls back.

Within minutes Becky is back and walking towards Jo. I growl and curl my lip.

"Why is she like this with me? Doesn't she know that I was the one who told you to get back down the rescue centre to save her life?" asks Becky looking sad.

"Penny Pops has had a very hard life up until now. She hasn't had many people who have been kind to her and is one very insecure dog. Sadly, she has had no choice but to learn to defend herself from getting hurt", replies Jo.

"But I don't understand, why has she bonded so closely with you and not even given me a chance to bond with her?" asks Becky.

"Penny and I connected the first day we met. She has a close bond with me as she trusts me. It is going to take time for her to trust you Becky. Dogs can read facial expressions and body language. Maybe you remind her of someone who has hurt her before? They have a very important bonding hormone called oxycontin which makes them feel good when they are shown love, care and understanding. It is still early days, we just need to be patient", Jo tells Becky.

"I know, but it is so frustrating. I want to be able to cuddle her like you do. Surely she knows I would never hurt her?" replies Becky.

"Becky, building up trust takes time. For now, you just need to closely watch her body language. If she shows the white of her eyes, starts to lick her lips, tenses her body or lays her ears back, you need to back away from her slowly and immediately turn your back. Don't forget, no eye contact for now. Make sure you take a deep breath in, as this will make you both feel nice and relaxed when you are near each other. Dogs can easily pick up on our energy and sometimes if you feel up tight with work for example, they will sense it and start to feel it too. I think it may help if you feed her in the evenings from now on, as this will strengthen the bond over time", says Jo.

"I have a blonde wig upstairs. Do you think it would help if I wore that, so my hair is the same colour as yours?" asks Becky, sounding slightly happier than earlier.

"It is worth a go", grins Jo.

Chapter 30

* * *

"Becky quickly, where are you?" Jo shouts out, as she finally finishes a conversation with someone on the phone.

"Are you ok?" asks Becky, as she comes flying up the stairs with Jacob close behind her.

"That was the vet Becky, and guess what?" grins Jo.

"Tell me. Hurry up, please tell me", pleads Becky.

"Penny Pops is ok. The biopsy has come back all clear. The vet has put it down to a build-up of stress after everything she has been through which had caused the large mass to appear on her lymph glands. She said if we continue to give her lots of tender loving care along with her medication, the lump should disappear altogether in another week or so. How awesome is this?" cries out Jo, who I notice has tears running down her face.

"I am so relieved Jo", replies Becky, as I see tears running down her face too.

This sounds awesome news to me, and I am assuming their tears are ones of happiness.

Jo gets up and I watch as she goes over to give Becky a hug.

"I can't wait to tell Mum and Dad. I will call them now", I hear Becky say before disappearing.

"What awesome news is this Jacob? Penny is going to be fine. Give me a high five", she tells him.

I watch as Jacob immediately obliges. He lifts his right paw and touches Jo's hand with it and for the first time ever, he turns and winks at me.

'Wow, I never expected that', I think to myself, suddenly feeling very happy.

I did laugh to myself yesterday as I watched Becky walking around wearing a blonde wig. She must think I am daft, as I know it is still her.

"Come on Penny Pops, let's get ready and go for a celebration walk", grins Jo, as she bends down to give me a big kiss.

I follow her down the stairs and I laugh as Daisy play bows to me with her bottom high up into the air.

I turn around as fast as I can and dart back up the stairs to hide under Jo's desk.

Inside A Dog's Mind

I can hear Daisy is not far away. She is in hot pursuit so I stay as still as I possibly can.

'Woof', she tells me, as I suddenly see her cute little face looking at me from under the desk.

I quickly run into the bedroom with Daisy hot on my tail once again.

I laugh as Daisy jumps onto the bed and tosses all four pillows onto the floor with her nose. Her tail is wagging one hundred miles per hour and she has a very mischievous look in her eyes.

I run down the stairs and accidently bump into Jacob, who immediately growls and nips my bottom in anger.

Daisy flies past him too and he also tells her off.

"Look at you two having such fun girls. It is so lovely to see you playing together", says Jo, as she appears from out of the kitchen.

'Woof, woof, woof', Jacob tells her.

"What is the matter Jacob? Why don't you want to play?" Jo asks him.

'Woof, woof, woof', he continues.

"Come here you, my Mr Needy", says Jo, as she bends down and holds her arms open wide.

He wiggles his bum and literally sits on top of Jo. To be honest, he is a very needy dog. Every opportunity he gets, he sits on top of Becky or Jo and demands their attention. If they stop stroking him, can you believe he has the cheek to pick up their hand in his mouth and moves it where he wants them to stroke him next?

"Becky can you put their harnesses on whilst I just return a call", Jo calls out.

"Sure", she replies.

I watch as Becky gets Daisy and Jacob ready.

"Come on Penny, your turn now", she tells me with a warm smile.

'Grrrr', I tell her, as I start to lick my lips and get ready to lunge at her.

Becky immediately turns around and now has her back to me. Jacob instantly stands in front of her curling his lip and growling at me.

I growl back.

"What on earth is going on here?" asks Jo, as she comes flying around the corner.

I back off from Jacob and wag my tail at her.

"Are you ok Becky?" asks Jo.

"I am ok, just a little shaken that's all. Penny is a bit like Jekyll and Hyde. Her mood can change at the click of a finger and I still don't know how to read her body language", says Becky, sounding frustrated.

"Oh Becky, I am so sorry you're feeling shaken up. Penny Pops, now please listen to me. You need to be nice to Becky, do you hear me?" Jo says, as she bends over to put on my harness.

I do feel bad, as Becky hasn't done anything to hurt me, but Jo is my favourite person ever and I don't want to share her with anyone. I know it sounds selfish, but I can't help how I feel. I decide to try my best to control my outbursts, although sometimes I can't stop myself and then unfortunately it is often too late.

Chapter 31

* * *

"Penny Pops. I am thrilled to see the lump has finally disappeared. It has taken just over three weeks, but we got there in the end baby, didn't we?" Jo grins at me, as she finishes grooming my soft and silky coat.

I love being groomed, but only by Jo. I always groom her back with my tongue by licking the soft skin on her bare arms. She constantly giggles and tells me it tickles her.

"Becky, we are going to have to do a road walk today, as it is literally pouring down outside", Jo shouts out.

"I cannot believe it is raining in June. At least it's warm rain", calls back Becky.

"Looks like you are going to have a bath in the rain now Penny", laughs Jo, as I follow her down the stairs.

The five of us set off up the driveway. The rain feels nice and cooling on my back as we turn to the right, continuing to follow the pavement.

Inside A Dog's Mind

I suddenly have a panic attack. I hear a car slamming on its brakes as it goes past us and the swishing sound of water instantly hurts my head. I lunge out into the road to protect Jo, as the memories of my accident return to haunt me.

Jo looks to be taken by surprise and quickly reins me in.

"Blimey Jo, that was close. I have never seen Penny do that before", says Becky, who is walking behind us with Jacob and Daisy.

"Me neither Becky. She did seem rather anxious", replies Jo, as I another car flies by throwing water towards us.

I immediately lunge again towards the road.

"Hey Penny Pops. It's ok. What is the matter baby?" asks Jo, as she leans over to look at me.

I so wish I could tell her all about that dreadful night.

Another car goes by and I lunge again.

"Becky let's walk over to the fields. You might think I am mad, but I have just had a picture appear in my head. I am sure the night Penny got hit by the car, it must have been raining. In fact, this makes complete sense. This is the first time we have had any rain since she came to live with us", Jo tells Becky.

'How on earth does Jo manage to read my mind like this?' I think to myself in awe.

Michelle Holland

"You could be right", replies Becky, as we head down a quiet footpath towards the fields ahead.

I immediately start to relax and let out a huge sigh of relief.

I drop my ball at Jo's feet. She immediately picks it up and throws it into the distance. Jacob chases after my ball and gets to it just before I do. He picks it up and walks around with my ball in his mouth like he is a king to tease me. It isn't long before he gets bored and drops my ball so we can start all over again.

Jacob has also started playing with me inside the house, but only on his terms. A fun game we play in the evening is when I sit on the sofa and push one of the balls with my nose across the lounge towards him. He immediately picks it up, drops it onto Jo's lap, she gives it to me, and we start all over again. Daisy never joins in, as she is always asleep relaxing with her legs up in the air. I will tell you though, if I push my ball in the wrong direction and it goes too near her sofa, she jumps off like a rocket and heads towards me looking angry with her teeth showing and our game is immediately over.

Daisy is always on a lunge line when we go out for walks across the fields, as apparently, she has taken quite a liking to sheep and cannot contain her excitement when she sees them. Thankfully, she does get to run free when we all visit the secure field though. I love going to this field, as different human friends of Jo and Becky's also come along with their dogs too and we have great fun chasing each other and playing ball. The humans I am relieved to say don't pay me any attention and never give me any eye contact which makes me feel at ease.

"I wonder how Penny will react when she sees David, Harry and Emma later. Do you think she will remember them?" Becky asks Jo, as we head back down our driveway.

'I haven't a clue who Becky is talking about. I don't know any humans with those names', I think to myself.

"It will be very interesting to see Becky. Dog's never ever forget someone who has shown kindness to them. Thankfully, Claire managed to get his telephone number for me, as she knew how much he loved Penny Pops. Oh Becky, David couldn't believe it when I called him to tell him we have got Penny Pops safe at home with us. He was totally shocked as he'd thought the rescue had followed through with the PTS appointment and out of principle he hasn't been back there ever since", replies Jo.

"Oh, Penny Pops, you are so pretty. Look at Penny's ears Becky, they have gone all crinkly and curly from the rain. How cute does she look?" says Jo, as she rubs me all over with a soft clean towel.

"Aw Jo, she looks gorgeous. What time is David popping over?" replies Becky.

"In about an hour. I said I would meet him at the top of the driveway so he can say hello. If all goes well, maybe he could come in and have a cuppa with us all. What do you think?" says Jo.

"That's sounds like a great idea. It would certainly be nice to meet him. Is he bringing his two children? Do you know how old they are?" asks Becky.

"I am not sure to be honest. We will soon find out though. Would you be able to get three cheese Kong's ready? This will keep them occupied if he does pop in", grins Jo.

'I am very intrigued to who these humans could be', I think to myself.

Chapter 32

✳ ✳ ✳

"Right let me get your harness on so we can go and meet David", Jo tells me, as she gets up from her desk.

"Good luck", calls Becky, as we head off out through the side door.

I am pleased to see it has finally stopped raining, as we make our way out through the back gate.

I immediately stand with my nose high into the air. I notice a very tall man and two smaller humans standing at the top of the drive.

We slowly start to walk towards them.

"Penny Pops", shouts the man, as he starts trotting towards me with his arms open wide.

'I seriously cannot believe this. It is my human and his two puppies who used to come and take me out for walks at the prison', I suddenly realise.

I run to him as fast as I can and literally jump into his arms.

"I cannot tell you how good it is to see you my girl", he tells me, as he continues to hold me tight.

'I am finding it hard to take all of this in. I didn't think I would ever see them again', I say to myself, feeling slightly emotional.

"Look Penny Pops, Harry and Emma have come to see you too", says David, as he gently places me back down.

My bum is wriggling so fast. It is so good to see my little humans again. I kiss Emma first and then a slobbery one for Harry. They are both grinning as they continue to make a big fuss of me.

"I can't believe you used to call her Penny Pops too", smiles Jo, as she slowly wipes a tear from her eyes.

"I can't believe they were going to kill her. Evil people Thank you for saving her", blurts out Emma.

'Kill who? Maybe she is talking about one of the characters in a story David has told her', I think to myself.

"Hey Emma, it is nice to meet you, Harry and your Dad at last. Would you like to come in and meet Becky and our other two rescues?" Jo asks.

'Please say yes', I plead.

"You have more dogs? We love dogs and all animals, don't we Harry?" answers Emma.

Harry nods in agreement.

"Come on then, follow me", Jo says, as we walk back down the driveway.

I can't help myself and keep jumping up at David, continuously trying kiss him.

"How amazing is this", grins Jo, as she hands David my lead.

"David, Emma and Harry. Meet Becky, Jacob and Daisy", says Jo, as we all head into the lounge.

I stay closely by David's side, as Harry fusses Jacob and Emma sits on the floor next to Daisy.

"Daisy is just like a Disney dog", coos Emma.

I don't even notice that Jo has disappeared until she returns with drinks for everyone.

"And how old are you and Harry?" Becky is asking.

"I am six years old and Harry is eight. He likes to boss me around", replies Emma in a very cute voice.

"Mummy used to come and walk Penny with us sometimes too", pipes up Harry.

"Maybe we could all meet up for a walk over the Downs sometime?" asks Becky.

'How awesome would this be? I would love to see them all again', I smile to myself.

Michelle Holland

"Becky, you should have seen Penny Pops when she first saw David. She literally jumped up into his arms. I have never seen her bum wag so fast", beams Jo.

"Look she hasn't left his side", smiles Becky.

"Maybe now and again, I could come and take Penny Pops to the beach with me. You'd like that my girl, wouldn't you?" David asks me.

'Woof', I reply.

"So, the plan is, you are fostering her then?" says David to Jo.

"Yes David, three dogs in the house permanently is a definite no. Also, Penny keeps growling and lunging at me. I can't even stroke her, and she has now been here for over one month", Becky butts in.

"It takes time Becky. Maybe you remind her of someone who has been horrible to her. Just give her some space and let her come to you in her own time", he replies.

'I don't ever want to leave here. I must make an extra effort to be nicer to Becky', I tell myself sternly.

"Right kiddoes, time for us to make a move", says David, as he starts to get up.

'No, I want you to stay here too', I cry out.

"Bye, bye Penny Pops. See you soon", says Emma wrapping her arms tightly around my neck.

"Oh Emma. How sweet is that? I would love to be able to give Penny a hug like that", says Becky, sounding slightly sad.

"You will one day Becky, trust me", replies Jo.

"I'll message you later Jo, so we can get a walking date in the diary", says David, as he gently plants a kiss onto the top of my head

I watch feeling happy, as the humans start to hug each other. Jacob and Daisy get a hug from David, Harry and Emma too.

"See you soon, my girl and make sure you are nice to Becky", he tells me, before heading out of the door with my two little puppies by his side.

Chapter 33

* * *

Two weeks have gone by and can you believe we have even met up with David and his family twice now already.

I've also tried to be on my best behaviour with Becky. One evening, I even walked across to her and leaned my body against her legs. She'd gently stroked me for a few seconds, which I allowed and when I'd had enough, I just took myself off to lie down on my bed. Becky and Jo seemed to be elated.

One evening Jo's two human sons came over for dinner. It was the first time I'd met them. I instantly liked them both as they looked very similar to Jo and both had wonderful calm energies. They even saved Jacob, Daisy and me some of the chicken from their dinner. *How cool is this?* I had never heard four humans laugh as much as they did that night. The room had been full of warmth and love. I also had my photo taken with them both too.

"Jo, you really snored badly last night, and I hardly got any sleep at all. Sometimes I think you stop breathing. I think you need to get a doctor's appointment to check you haven't got that sleep apnoea thingy. Tonight, I am going to sleep in the spare room. I feel like a walking Zombie", says Becky.

'I don't like the sound of Jo stopping breathing. I shall make sure I keep a closer eye on her from now on', I think to myself.

"Ok, I will try and get an appointment for next week. I am sorry I was snoring so badly that it kept you awake Becky", says Jo.

"Don't forget Mum and Dad will be over shortly", replies Becky.

I wonder who they could be?

"Remember Mum, Dad, no eye contact with Penny", says Becky, as two new humans appear through the front door.

"Hey Jacob, my boy", says the man, as I watch Jacob jump up and down in excitement.

I have never seen him so excited.

Daisy is squealing and kissing the new lady. She seems elated to see them both.

"Nana and Grandad have missed you so much", says the lady, as she pulls out a bag of delicious smelling treats.

"One for you Jacob, one for you Daisy. Penny would you like one?" I hear I ask.

I immediately rush over to where the lady is sitting.

"Gently Penny Pops", Jo tells me.

"No eye contact Mum", repeats Becky, sounding slightly anxious.

I gently take the treat.

"Good girl Penny Pops. Go and find your ball", Jo tells me.

I stand back and watch as they sit chatting and laughing in the kitchen.

'They seem like nice people, especially as they brought us treats too', I think to myself.

"Right, who is going to come and help Nana and Grandad in the garden?" asks the new lady.

'Woof', replies Jacob, as he jumps off his bed and wags his half a tail.

I hope someone will explain to me one day how he lost half his tail, as that must have been very painful.

I follow everyone outside into the garden and watch intrigued as they start removing weeds from out of the soil from around all the plants.

I drop my ball at the man's feet who seems to be called Grandad and wait patiently for him to see it.

"Is this your ball Penny?" he asks me, with a warm smile on his face.

I crouch down low and wait for him to throw it.

"Ready, steady, go", he calls, as my ball flies across the garden.

I race off as quickly as I can to retrieve it and drop it back down by his feet.

Off we go again, as he continues to throw my ball. He throws, I fetch. I like Grandad.

"Aren't you tired yet?" he asks me,

"Penny will play until she drops", laughs Jo.

"I love her colouring, she is very striking and beautiful", says the lady called Nana.

"How long is she staying with you for?" asks Grandad.

"Until we can find her the right home. She needs to be with one human who maybe has another dog for company", replies Becky.

'I suddenly stop in my tracks. What are they talking about? I don't want to go and live anywhere else. I want to stay here with my Jo', I think to myself, feeling slightly anxious.

"I have had a lady contact me. She is not only a behaviourist, but is a qualified dog walker, owns her own business and sadly lost her eleven-year old collie recently. She lives in Crawley and I've told her I will try and visit her in the week to do a home check," says Jo, in a very sad voice.

'Nooooo', I cry out, as I sit down next to Jo.

Jo turns to wrap her arms around me and kisses me gently on the top of my head.

"You have really bonded with her Jo, haven't you?" says Grandad, in a very soft voice.

"I fell in love with her the first day I saw her and want to keep her more than anything", replies Jo.

"We have been through this Jo. It is just not practical having three dogs to look after", says Becky, in a very firm voice.

I look up into Jo's eyes to see they are filled with tears and mine start to well up too.

"Come on let's go back inside and have a quick drink before we head off home", says Nana, as she quickly puts all the gardening tools safely back into the shed.

I lie in the kitchen listening to them chat. Jacob has his head on Grandad's lap.

"Right, let me just wash these cups up, before we make a move. Hey Penny, are you ok?" asks Nana, as I roll over on my back to expose my tummy.

Suddenly she leans over and all I see is her hand coming towards me. I immediately go into defence mode and growl loudly at her. She jumps back in surprise, as I get ready to lunge.

"Oh no you don't", says Jo, as she grabs me by my collar.

"Are you ok Mum?" Becky is asking her, looking very concerned.

"Well I wasn't expected that. I thought she wanted me to rub her belly. That was very close", Nana replies.

"See Jo, she is too unpredictable. I will not put Mum at risk. You had better get that home check done pronto. Do you hear me?" says Becky, in quite a harsh voice.

"I am ok", replies Nana quickly.

I can see tears running down Jo's face, as she holds me close to her.

'I have let Jo down', I say to myself, feeling very ashamed.

Chapter 34

∗ ∗ ∗

"Well, how did it go?" asks Becky, as Jo arrives back home.

I am so pleased to see Jo and cannot contain my excitement. I have been lying patiently by the front door waiting for her to return.

"She seemed nice enough. Across the road from where she lives, there are fifty acres of private fields which belong to her family. She liked the photos I showed her, and she is going to come on a walk with us at three o'clock today. I have filled out the home visit form and seen all her qualifications. She seems experienced enough and has a calm energy. If all goes ok, she said she would like to take her on one week's trial", replies Jo, sounding very sad.

"It is for the best", says Becky.

I follow Jo up the stairs and she hugs me tight.

"Me and you have got to be very brave later. Do you hear me?" Jo is asking me, with tears rolling down her face.

I am feeling confused. I don't like seeing Jo cry like this. Is this all my fault?

"Right my Penny Pops. We need to pack a few of your toys and some food, just in case", she tells me.

'I don't want to go anywhere without you', I cry out.

"Good luck Jo. Bye Penny", calls Becky, as me and Jo make our way out to her car.

"I want you to be nice to this lady we are about to meet. She can give you the one to one attention you so deserve", Jo tells me, as we arrive at one of my favourite walking places.

I watch as she slowly gets out of the car and greets a small looking lady who has the same hair colour as me.

"Come on Penny Pops. It is time for you to meet Jade", Jo tells me, as I jump out of the car.

"Remember Jade, no eye contact with her at all. Please let her come to you in her own time", Jo continues.

I watch as the new lady nods and we set off on our walk.

"She really is a truly stunning looking collie Jo", I hear Jade say.

"I totally agree. I fell in love with her the first moment I laid eyes on her", Jo replies.

"I am not surprised. How long did it take her to bond like this with you?" asks Jade.

"We bonded immediately, but it is now over two months and she still hasn't bonded with Becky yet. That is why I am feeling under pressure, as it isn't helping Penny Pops with the two of us rowing", Jo says, sounding sad.

'I feel bad for Jo. She is only trying to do what everyone thinks is the best thing for all of us, but I know splitting the two of us up, is not going to help. Me and Jo deserve to be together forever', I think, as a lump appears in my throat.

"Why don't you throw Penny Pops some treats?" asks Jo.

I immediately drop my ball and chase after the scattered treats Jade has just thrown down onto the grass in front of me.

'Now I must say, these really do taste delicious', I say to myself, as I eagerly wait for more.

"Can you catch?" Jade asks me, as I watch a treat fly towards me.

"Fabulous catch Penny Pops", calls out Jo, who has a huge grin across her face.

"Wow, she is very fast", says Jade, as another treat lands on the grass to my left.

"Why not throw the ball for her? She's always one hundred per cent focussed when her ball is around. By the way, she also enjoys playing hide and seek too", says Jo.

"I run quite a few dog training courses alongside my behaviourist work and dog walking, so she will be with me at all times", smiles Jade.

'I am not really sure about any of this', I think to myself, as I drop the ball back at Jo's feet.

"Penny Pops. Why not push your ball to Jade?" she asks me.

I immediately lie down and push the ball with my nose. I feel proud when it lands safely at Jade's feet.

"That was awesome Penny. You are such a clever girl, aren't you?" praises Jade.

"She is the most intelligent and loyal dog I have ever known. She picks up things really quickly", Jo tells her, looking at me in a very lovingly way.

"I am prepared to give it a go. Why not start off with the week's trial like you suggested and then we can go from there?" asks Jade.

'Noooooo', I cry out.

"Will you promise to message me and send photos regularly?" says Jo.

"Of course, I will", Jade assures her.

"Please make sure you let her settle in before you introduce her to any new people. She gets anxious if she is overwhelmed too quickly", Jo tells her.

"Don't you worry Jo. I will take it very slowly with her and if I come across any problems, I will immediately let you know, and anyway we are only half an hour's drive away" replies Jade.

"That's true. I have some of her food and toys in the car. Just to warn you, she likes to destroy any toy which has a squeak inside. Penny Pops loves to have her teddy bear close to her, as this is her favourite comfort toy", says Jo.

I walk closely by Jo's side, feeling worried and confused as we make our way back to the car.

I watch as Jo opens the back door and I immediately try to jump in.

"No Penny Pops. You are going on an adventure with Jade. I want you to promise me you will be a good girl. I will come and visit you real soon. Remember, I love you", she tells me, with tears in her eyes.

'I don't want to go anywhere with her', I scream out.

"Come on, jump up into Jade's boot with teddy", she tells me.

I totally refuse to move, as I try to get my paws to stick firmly on the ground. Suddenly, I feel myself being picked up and Jo gently places me in the boot of this strange car. The boot is shut and me and Teddy are trapped.

Tears roll down my face, as I watch Jo turn away. Her shoulders look to be shaking up and down, as she gets into her car.

'Noooooo. Come back Jo, I love and need you', I scream out, as the car starts to move, and my Jo completely disappears out of sight.

My heart is truly broken.

Chapter 35

*　*　*

I LISTEN TO THE MUSIC *playing in the car, as I wrap by paws tightly around Teddy.*

'I cannot believe this is happening. Is this all my fault?' I keep asking myself, over and over again.

'I need to come up with an escape plan as soon as possible, so I can get back to my Jo', I think, as I start to feel a little more hopeful.

The car suddenly grinds to a halt.

"We are home", I hear Jade's voice telling me.

I wait patiently for the boot to open.

Jade is smiling down at me.

I curl up my lip and growl.

'This is the person who has taken me away from my Jo', I think to myself, feeling very angry.

"We will have none of that behaviour thank you", Jade tells me, as she instructs me to jump out of the car.

Inside A Dog's Mind

I watch as she closes the boot.

'Teddy, I need my Teddy', I cry out.

"Come on, this way", she tells me, as we walk up a garden path to a wooden door.

I peak my head inside to have a look around. It all looks completely different to my old house.

"Right, I will get you a drink and then you can have an explore around", she tells me, as she unclips my lead.

I can smell lots of other dog's scents in here, but I can't see any at all.

'I miss Jacob, Daisy and Becky too', I suddenly say to myself.

"This is the lounge where you will sleep", she tells me.

'Why am I not sleeping upstairs? I do not like the sound of this. I am not used to sleeping on my own', I think, as I start to panic.

"Through this door is the garden. What do you think?" she asks me

I decide to take a peak outside. The garden is very big and there are lots of trees all the way around the outside. I have a good old sniff around, followed by a very long wee.

"If you follow me, I'll show you upstairs, but you won't be allowed up there very often. Only as a treat now and again", she continues.

Michelle Holland

'I don't like the sound of this', I say, as I look inside each room.

Suddenly, I hear a noise coming from downstairs.

I put my nose high into the air. I stand still and rigid. I am instantly on guard. I can smell an imposter.

"Jade are you there?" shouts out a deep gruff voice.

I am shocked to see a large stranger with a huge beard standing at the bottom of the stairs.

'Grrrr, woof, grrrr, woof', I call out, with my body poised and my teeth showing.

"Dad. What on earth are you doing here. I told you not to come around, didn't I?" shouts Jade, who looks to be as shocked as me to see this man standing there.

"But I wanted to meet your new dog", he replies, as I slowly take two steps towards him.

I growl as loudly as I can with my lip curled tightly.

"Dad, back off now", shouts Jade, as she manages to grab my harness just in time to stop me from lunging down the stairs after him.

"What on earth have you got there? What were you thinking taking on a vicious dog? Your Mum is going to go spare", he shouts back.

"That is why I told you not to come around Dad. I needed to give her time to settle in. Why didn't you just listen to me? Thanks to you, she's in a right state now. Can you just go into the garden out of the way whilst I put her lead on? I'll take her for a walk to try and calm her down", replies Jo, sounding pretty angry.

I continue to show my teeth and growl.

Once the man has disappeared, I finally stop. I pant loudly, as I try to calm myself down.

'I want to go home to my Jo with Teddy', I cry out to myself.

"You have got yourself all worked up, haven't you? Have a little drink and I'll then take you for a little walk", Jade tells me.

'I need to be on my guard in case that man appears out of nowhere again', I tell myself.

I lap up the water, keeping one ear alert.

"This way", Jade tells me, as she opens the front door.

I put my nose high into the air. I can sense he is still around somewhere.

I growl again as I check to the left and the right.

I feel constantly on edge as we walk down a quiet country lane. I keep looking behind me to check we are not being followed.

Suddenly, I hear a lot of shouting and screaming. A loud whistling sound hurts my ears. It reminds me of the night of my accident. From out of nowhere two metal spokes come whizzing towards me at great speed. I lunge as high as I can, but it is gone in a flash.

"Penny, please calm down", Jade is telling me, sounding very anxious.

I am panting hard and feeling very fearful. I just need to get out of here. I can't help myself as I lunge at a man who is jogging straight towards me. I narrowly miss his leg, as Jade struggles to keep me under control.

I jump and bark, as she tries to pull me away from all the noisy activity ahead.

I continue to leap and lunge for all I am worth.

'Where is my Jo?' I cry out, feeling totally insecure and untrusting.

My body is tense as Jade tries to stroke me.

'Grrrrr', I tell her, curling my lip tightly.

"I cannot cope with you Penny. You scare me. I am going to phone Jo straight away", she tells me, as she opens the car boot and asks me to jump in.

I refuse and turn to growl at her.

She quickly throws some treats into the car. I jump in and I am so thrilled to see Teddy waiting for me.

Chapter 36

* * *

'Ring, ring', I hear.

"Hello, Jo speaking", I suddenly hear.

That's my Jo', I call out, as I eagerly look around for her.

"It's Jade".

"Is Penny Pops ok?", says Jo, sounding very worried.

"Yes, she is but I am not. I am pretty shaken up. She is a crazy dog", replies Jade.

I am confused, as I cannot see Jo anywhere.

"What do you mean? What on earth has happened? You've only had her for three hours" Jo says.

"My Dad appeared in the house when I told him not to visit and it set Penny off into a wild frenzy. She stood at the top of the stairs, continuing to growl and lunging fiercely at him. I then struggled to get her out of the house and took her down to the park. That is when she went crazy. She was lunging like a lunatic at bikes and joggers. She also growled at me", Jade tells her.

"I thought you were going to have two quiet weeks, with just you and her. You are supposed to be a trained behaviourist. Why on earth did you put her in situations that you knew she wouldn't feel comfortable in? I am completely lost for words", Jo replies angrily.

"Jade, where is Penny now?" I suddenly hear Becky's voice.

I look around, but I can't see her either.

"She is in the boot of my car. I cannot cope with her, so I am bringing her back to you right now", says Jade

'Did I just hear right? I am going home to my Jo', I think, feeling totally uplifted.

"Ok. Calm down Jade. How about we meet you both half-way? We now want Penny back as soon as possible too. Do you know the layby outside the school at Chailey?" replies Becky.

'Go Becky', I say to myself.

She has most definitely gone up in my estimations.

"Yes, I do. Ok I will see you there shortly. I am sorry for all the hassle", says Jade.

Everything goes quiet.

'Where have Jo and Becky gone?' I wonder to myself.

It isn't long until we come to a halt.

I sit and look out of the window, but I can only see cars driving past.

Why are we sitting here?

Suddenly, I see a car approaching and it pulls up just behind us. It looks familiar, but I cannot think why.

'OMG, OMG', *I shout out, as I see Jo and Becky walking towards me.*

I bark as loud as I can. Am I dreaming? Is this real?

Jade get's out of the car.

"You can get her out Jo. I am not going near her", I hear Jade say.

Suddenly the boot opens.

I cannot tell you how happy I feel, as I see Jo's smiling face looking down at me. She has tears in her eyes, and I jump up into her open arms. I lick her face and cannot stop my body from wriggling with excitement.

"Hi Penny", grins Becky.

I am so pleased to see her, so I decide to kiss her too.

"Come on, let me get Teddy and then we can all go home", says Becky, as she grins at Jo's happy face.

Daisy is absolutely thrilled to see me. I jump into the back seat next to her and I smile as her tail wags in a very crazy manner, as she tries to lick my face. Jacob looks at me and winks.

I cannot tell you how happy I am feeling at this precise moment.

"Sorry about this once again", I hear Jade say, as she hands the rest of my stuff to Jo.

"I just hope you haven't set Penny back too far and may I suggest you retrain yourself before you call yourself a behaviourist. I am disgusted with what has gone on, you are experienced enough to know better", replies Jo, sounding very angry.

"Leave it Jo. We have Penny back and thankfully she is safe, which is the main thing", Becky tells her, as they both get into the car.

"We are going home", sings Jo, as she turns to look at me.

Our eyes connect and that warm fuzzy feeling instantly returns through every part of my body.

How awesome is this?

I am thrilled when we pull up outside Jo and Becky's house. I jump out of the car and rush towards the door.

"Steady baby girl. It looks like you are pleased to be back home", laughs Jo.

Daisy and Jacob chase me into the lounge. I jump onto the sofa and Daisy follows. Jacob fetches me a ball. I jump off, pick it up and push it to him.

"Look Penny, here is Teddy", Becky tells me, as she places him on the floor next to me.

I am not quick enough. Jacob pounces on him, grabs him in his mouth and flies up the stairs at a very fast speed. I chase after him in hot pursuit, and then stop instantly as I see Jo.

I slowly walk towards her wagging my tail in happiness. She sits down next to me and holds me tight.

"I know you were only gone for three hours, but I really missed you. I love you Penny Pops", she whispers.

Chapter 37

* * *

"That was really bizarre what happened last night", I hear Jo say to Becky.

"Why? Tell me more", replies Becky.

"Well, I was having this really weird dream. We were flying to Hong Kong in a toilet of all things and I couldn't get out. I started to panic and scream loudly. The next thing I knew, Penny Pops was pawing at me, trying to wake me up", says Jo.

"I know you dream a lot and hold your breath. It sounds like Penny was concerned and sensed something was wrong and knew she needed to wake you up. How clever is she?" smiles Becky.

"Maybe Penny Pops is acting as my therapy dog. It will be interesting to see what the sleep clinic tells me when I go there at the end of August. When I woke up, Penny was right next to me with her head on your pillow looking so darn cute", laughs Jo.

"She is very cute. By the way, I need to know what you want for your birthday next week?" she asks Jo.

"You know what I want Becky. The best birthday present in the whole wide world, would be for Penny Pops to stay here forever", Jo replies.

"Every time I ask you, that is what you reply. I cannot tell you how many times you have said this to me Jo, we need to be sensible, although there is something I need to confess to you", says Becky, in a very serious tone.

"What?" asks Jo, immediately looking worried.

"Well I organised this months ago, before Penny arrived into our lives. I have booked us a four day stay in a log cabin in Derbyshire. It was supposed to be a surprise for your birthday", says Becky.

"OMG really?" blurts out Jo.

"Yes, but the only trouble is, they only allow a maximum of two dogs" continues Becky.

"Nooo", groans Jo, as I watch her face drop.

"But", she says with a pause. "I spoke to them earlier and explained all about Penny. Can you believe they have agreed to let us take her too? How cool is this?" shouts out Becky.

Michelle Holland

"OMG, I cannot believe it. The five of us are going on holiday. Jacob, Daisy, Penny Pops, did you hear this?" calls out Jo, as she dances around in circles, before giving Becky a big hug.

Me, Jacob and Daisy decide to join in with all this excitement. We jump up and bark, as Becky and Jo continue to dance around.

I smile as so much love and happiness fills the room.

"Oh, and by the way Jo, I have managed to book a one to one session next Tuesday at two o'clock with a local fly ball trainer. It is just for me and Penny. I felt it might do us both good to spend some quality time together, that is if it is ok with you?" asks Becky.

Jo's face is beaming, as she rushes over once again to Becky, but this time gives her a high five.

'Um, I thought only dogs do high fives', I say to myself.
I have never been on holiday. How exciting Is this?

"Right guys. Let me get some work done and then we can start making a list of what we need to pack for our holiday", grins Jo.

"Jo we are not going until next Friday so there is plenty of time to write a list", laughs Becky.

"I know, but I am so excited. Jacob, Daisy and Penny Pops can each take a small suitcase with their favourite toys in and Teddy can come too", says Jo, as she looks across at me.

"You are like a big kid even though you are going to be forty-nine soon. I will send you the link to where we are going, so you can check it out", replies Becky.

"I am young at heart Becky. It is just my body that lets me down now and again", says Jo.

I follow Jo up to her office and sit under her desk with my head on her lap.

"Ok Penny Pops. Let's have a look at where we are going on holiday, before I start on my work", I hear her tell me.

"Oh wow. This looks truly stunning. The log cabin has three bedrooms and is situated in the centre of the beautiful Peak District. A lounge with TV, bathroom and a hot tub. Enjoy the fantastic views from the raised decking area, a local grocery store on sight and numerous local pubs within a five-mile radius. From the high, moorland plateaus in the north, to the steep-sided, deep dales and rolling green hills in the south of the area, the Peak District and Derbyshire has just about any landscape you can imagine in Britain, making it one of the finest areas in the country to go walking", she continues.

Michelle Holland

'*I must say I am liking the sound of this*', *I say to myself, starting to feel a tad excited.*

"I am going to find it hard to concentrate on my work now", laughs Jo, as she looks down into my eyes.

I wag my tail whilst she strokes the top of my head.

"Only eight days until we go on holiday Penny Pops", she smiles.

Chapter 38

* * *

"Jo, could you put Penny's harness on for me please?" calls Becky

"Give me two seconds", Jo replies.

'This is a bit bizarre, as we have already been out for a nice walk. I wonder where we are all going this time?' I think to myself.

"Are you looking forward to it?" Jo asks, as Becky appears.

"Too be honest, yes I am", she grins.

'I am confused as Becky has her trainers on ready, I have my harness on, but Jacob, Daisy and Jo don't seem to be getting ready. Why not?' I ask myself.

"Come on Penny", says Becky, as she takes hold of my lead.

I look back questioningly at Jo.

"Off you trot Penny Pops, go and have some fun with Becky. You will love it", she tells me, before closing the door.

I have no choice but to follow Becky and jump onto the back seat of Jo's car.

I look through the window, but there is no sign of Jo at all.

Becky sings along to the radio, as we take a ten-minute drive before pulling up by a large green field.

"Come on, out you get Penny. It is time for a bit of fly ball fun", she tells me, with a large grin.

Ahead I can see a man who looks to be setting up some very small jumps in a straight line and either side of them sits some mesh.

"Hi there, are you Shane?" calls out Becky.

"I certainly am. You must be Becky and Penny", he calls back.

"Remember Shane, no eye contact", she replies.

"Don't you worry. I am used to dealing with dogs who have issues. That is why flyball is so good for them. It gives them something to concentrate and focus on. Before we run through a few things, unclip Penny's lead and I will throw her a ball", says Shane.

"Are you sure?" asks Becky, sounding not overly convinced.

"Yes. Relax", he tells her.

I watch as Shane throws a ball at great speed to my left. I set off like a rocket in hot pursuit.

"Wow, she certainly has some speed", says Shane, as I return with the ball safely in my mouth.

"Now, the next step is to get her to drop the ball, as some dogs find it hard to give them up", he continues.

"Becky. I want you to get Penny's attention by calling her over to you whilst shaking this fleecy tug toy in the air", he tells her, as I watch him hand her something fluffy.

"Penny. Come", calls Becky, in a very low voice.

I look at her in a very strange way.

"Becky. Put some excitement into you voice. Come on, you can do a lot better than that", he tells her.

"Penny. Come and get it", she shouts out loudly, as she jumps up and down on the grass shaking around the furry thing.

This looks too inviting and I find it hard to resist. I drop my ball and dash over to retrieve the new toy.

"Now hold onto it and play tug", shouts Shane.

Becky pulls me and then I pull her. This is great fun.

"That's more like it. Becky, now bring her over to the start of the run. I will show her the ball and then walk to the other end. I want her totally focussed on the ball. Hold onto the back of her harness and when I tell you to go, you just release her. I want her to come and retrieve the ball from the board. It is then up to you to call her back with lots of excitement in your voice and when she clears the last jump, wave around the tug and hopefully she will drop the ball", he explains.

"But how do I get her to drop the tuggy before we start?" asks Becky.

"I am hoping that when I show her the ball, she will drop the tuggy and stay focussed on the ball. Shall we give it a go?" he asks.

"Let's do this", grins Becky.

To be honest I have never seen her this excited and enthusiastic. I like the new Becky.

"Look what I have got", Shane says to me, as he holds the ball right in front of my nose.

I immediately drop the tuggy and keep a very close eye on where Shane is taking the ball.

"Watch the ball Penny. Focus", Becky is telling me.

My adrenalin is building quickly, as Becky holds onto my harness.

"When you are ready", calls out Shane.

"Ready, steady, go get the ball Penny", shouts out Becky.

Inside A Dog's Mind

"Come on Penny", shouts out Shane, as I clear the first, the second, the third and the fourth jump easily. The ball is sitting on a piece of wooden board. I retrieve it on my first go.

"Penny. Bring the ball back to me", I hear Becky shout out loudly, as I turn and make my way back to her, clearing the obstacles with ease once again.

Becky is jumping up and down waving the tuggy at me.

I immediately drop the ball and me and Becky play tug once again.

'This is great fun', I say to myself, feeling very happy.

"Wasn't Penny just awesome", says Becky, sounding slightly out of breath, as Shane appears.

"For a dog who has never done this before, I am very impressed with her speed and quick learning. She could be a serious flyball dog in the making", he grins.

"Really?" replies Becky, sounding very proud.

"We will have a couple more goes in a moment, as I don't like to do too much on their first lesson. I just want to get them familiar with the way everything works. We can book in two more sessions like this and then if you want to, you can bring her regularly to our beginner's class on a Tuesday evening. It is in a huge indoor barn not far from here. Penny can then progress through the various stages and who knows, she may even be good enough one day to join our professional team", he smiles.

"This is so awesome. Penny I am so proud of you", beams Becky.

"She will also need an individual team member name", he tells her.

"Like what?" she asks.

"Well for instance we have dogs called Hurricane Henry, Feisty Flossy, Jack The Lad. It is entirely up to you", he replies.

"Penny does like to destroy most squeaky toys. I shall have a good old think on my way home", she smiles.

After two more fabulous games, I have a long drink of water and it isn't long before we are back in the car.

I am feeling completely exhausted after my exertions, but what great fun I've had.

"Come on. Let's go and tell them all about it", says Becky, as she unclips my seatbelt.

"How did it go?" asks Jo, as she comes to greet us, accompanied by Jacob and Daisy, who very annoyingly continue to sniff me all over.

"Penny is a real star in the making. I would like to introduce you all to, wait for it, The Dark Destroyer", beams Becky.

Becky laughs at Jo's puzzled face.

"This is her team member name for when she starts the real classes. How awesome is this?" she tells Jo.

"That is awesome. Wow, well done Penny Pops", says Jo, as she takes off my harness.

I decide to lie down whilst I listen to them chat away.

'Only three days left until we go on holiday', I think to myself, as my eyes start to close.

Chapter 39

*   *   *

"Are you sure we have got everything?" Jo asks Becky, as the final case is loaded into the back of Jo's car.

'I cannot believe today is the day we are going on holiday', I say to myself, feeling very excited.

"Yep, I think we have. We have their food, toys, beds, towels, our clothes and toiletries. We both have our laptops, although I seriously hope we won't have to do any work and to be honest I don't think we could fit anything else in the car even if we wanted to. It looks fit to bursting Jo and we are only going away for three nights", laughs Becky.

"Right. I will get Jacob, Penny pops and Daisy belted up safely in the back whilst you lock up. Then off we can all go on our holiday", grins Jo.

"We have a long journey ahead. It may take us four to five hours, but we can stop on the way as often as we need to so you can all have a wee. When we get there, we'll quickly unpack and then we can go out and explore the stunning countryside. Is that ok with you three?" she asks, as she leans over to clip on Daisy's seatbelt.

"Right, off we go then guys", calls out Becky, as the car starts to move.

"I am pleased we set off so early, as the traffic has been pretty kind to us so far. We are nearly half-way there", I hear Becky say.

I have been dozing and so have Jacob and Daisy.

"Does anyone need the toilet?" Jo asks.

'Woof, woof', replies Jacob.

"Ok. There is a service station in three miles. We can stop there, have a drink and stretch our legs", smiles Becky.

I have never been to a service station before.

"Come on, out you all get", says Jo, as she unclips our seatbelts and we all jump out.

'Ooh, this is so nice to have a good old stretch' I think to myself.

We take it in turns to have a wee and then a good old sniff around a large piece of grass. There are hundreds maybe thousands of different dog scents here. I have never smelt so many.

Michelle Holland

"Here we are. Have a drink before we all jump back into the car", says Becky, as she pours some lovely fresh water into one of our bowls.

It is gone in a jiffy, but thankfully she keeps topping it up.

"If you get them back in the car Jo, I'll just go and fill up their water bottle, pop to the toilet and grab us a coffee", says Becky, before she disappears.

It isn't long before we are back on the road and me, Jacob and Daisy settle down for another nap.

"Five minutes away", calls Jo.

The three of us sit up immediately.

'Wow. Just look at this beautiful countryside. It looks to run for miles and miles. Why can't I see any houses or humans around?' I think to myself.

"Now this is what I call a very rural and relaxing setting", sighs Becky, as we turn into a very long driveway.

To my left I can see little wooden houses dotted around and to the right sit's acres of open countryside.

"Jo. Can you read the instructions to where the key is hidden? The information is on the paperwork I printed off?" asks Becky.

"The cabin number is forty-two and there is a key safe to the right of the door. I have the code written down here", she replies.

"Ok. Look there is number twenty-four", says Becky.

"And there is number twenty-six, we are nearly there", Jo replies, sounding very excited.

"Here we are. Wow. Just look at this. How lucky are we to have the one right at the end? Look at the fabulous views we have", Becky says, as the car comes to a halt.

'I can't wait to go and explore', I say to myself.

"Jo. You go and find the key. I'll start to unload the car so we can get the luggage inside. Just stay there a little longer", Becky tells us.

As soon as the boot of the car opens, all three of our noses go high up into the air. There are so many inviting smells I need to check out.

"Right. Out you three come", says Jo, as one by one, we jump out.

Our noses are down on the ground in a jiffy and I laugh as Jacob immediately starts to mark his territory.

Daisy is busy squealing, as she has just seen a rabbit and is standing on her hind legs to see where it has gone.

It isn't long before we are inside the wooden house. It feels warm and homely. I wander outside onto the secure balcony and I smile as Daisy sits upright waiting for her new friend the rabbit to re-appear. At the end of the balcony is this huge round tub full of water. I have never seen anything like this before.

"We have finished unpacking, so let's get your harnesses back on. We can do some exploring and find somewhere to have dinner. I can't believe it is three o'clock already", Jo says.

"Where's Daisy?" asks Becky.

"Rabbit watching on the balcony", laughs Jo.

It isn't long before we are walking through this wonderful and stunning countryside.

"Becky, this is like something you would see on a postcard. It is so picturesque. The air smells clean and pure. Listen to the birds singing all around us. Truly awesome", says Jo.

Me and Jacob are not on our leads, but poor Daisy is staying on the lunge line. She is darting to the left and the right in her continuous search for rabbits. I nibble on some of the rabbit droppings along the way and Jacob copies me too. It seems such a long time since we had breakfast.

"According to this map, we need to turn right at the bottom of the field. We should then see a path that leads us down to the village", says Becky.

"Penny Pops, Jacob come here please. I need to put your leads on", calls Jo.

We immediately do as she asks and in return, we both get a very tasty treat.

"This is so pretty", gasps Becky, as we walk past some very quaint looking cottages.

A strong scent of rose petals fly up my nose and I can't help but sneeze.

"Bless you", Jo tells me.

"Look Becky. There is the pub over there and it looks to have a beautiful beer garden. Shall we eat here?" Jo asks.

"Yes, that sounds like a great idea. We can then head back so the dogs can have their dinner and I can pop to the local shop to get some bread and a few supplies. I may even jump into the hot tub later. We've all had a long day, being up so early and don't forget it's your birthday tomorrow,", replies Becky.

"I haven't forgotten Becky. Shall I go and order? Would you like your usual? I may get an extra piece of chicken to keep the babies occupied whilst we eat", says Jo.

'Now this sounds like a great idea to me', I say to myself.

It isn't long before an elderly looking lady brings out some food and I can smell the delicious aroma of chicken.

Michelle Holland

I watch drooling as Becky chops it up into tiny pieces and shares it between the three of us. It tastes awesome and is gone in no time at all.

"That was delicious", says Becky.

"I totally agree. Maybe we can come back here for my birthday dinner? It is such a lovely environment for the babies too", Jo replies, as she pours us a nice bowl of lovely fresh water.

"Yes, why not? Right let's make our way back now and I can pop to the shops whilst you get their dinner ready", says Becky, as she starts to get up.

The walk back to the wooden house was awesome. Daisy was in her element with all the little rabbits running around. Jacob stayed on his lead too, but I was free to roam, although I mainly stayed close by Jo's side.

I am not interested in chasing rabbits, I only chase balls.

I watch slightly concerned, as Jo climbs into the big round tub next to Becky. It starts to make a noise, so I jump up to see what on earth is happening.

"Hi Penny Pops", grins Jo.

There are hundreds of bubbles erupting from out of the water.

'Where did they come from?' *I think to myself, feeling puzzled.*

I stay rooted to where I am to make sure Jo is safe. Suddenly the noise stops, and all the bubbles disappear?

Where have they gone? By now I am totally confused.

"I am shattered", says Jo, as she climbs out of the tub.

"Me too", yawns Becky, as she starts to dry herself with a towel.

"I cannot believe it is ten o'clock already. Shall we take the dogs out for their last toilet and head off to bed?" asks Jo.

"Now that is a great idea. If you don't mind, I might sleep in the other bedroom. I need to get a good night's sleep tonight, as that was a long and draining drive today", replies Becky.

'Yippee, this means I will have Jo to myself', I shout out.

It isn't long before Jo is snuggled up in bed. Jacob and Daisy must have gone to sleep with Becky. I wait until Jo is fast asleep and as quietly as I can, I jump up onto the bed next to her.

She slowly rolls over and puts her right arm around me.
I feel warm and fuzzy once again.

'I am happiest I have ever felt', I think, as my eyes start to close.

Chapter 40

✶ ✶ ✶

"Wakey, wakey birthday girl", calls Becky, as she puts her head around the door.

I watch as she quickly pulls out her iPhone and takes a photo.

Jo has her arms wrapped around me and I have my head on the pillow next to her, as I wait for her to wake up.

"Happy birthday Jo", says Becky, in a slightly louder voice.

Jo starts to stir. She opens her eyes to see me looking at her and a huge smile starts to cover her face.

"Morning Penny Pops", she says to me.

"Birthday girl, I just took the cutest photo of you and Penny. I will show you once you are fully awake. I'll go and put the kettle on", says Becky, before disappearing.

Inside A Dog's Mind

To be honest, I am not at all sure what the word birthday means, but hopefully I will find out later.

"Up we get", Jo tells me, before she heads off to the bathroom.

I follow her closely. She sits on the bowl thing with her pyjama's around her ankles and I stand up on my hind legs at the other bowl. Jo leans over and turns on the tap and fresh water starts to flow.

"You do make me laugh Penny Pops", she tells me, with a smile.

"I bet you need the toilet too, don't you?" she asks me.

'Woof', I reply, as I follow her to the kitchen.

"Hey Jacob", she says, as he comes hurtling towards her. He receives a massive cuddle and seems happy to see me too.

"Daisy is already on rabbit duty. Shall we take them all for a quick toilet before we have our coffee? You can then open your presents and birthday cards", says Becky.

'Now this sounds interesting. I wonder what this is all about?' I think to myself.

"Ooh, I have presents?" replies Jo, sounding very excited.

"Yes, you do. I haven't written your card yet, so you can have that later", says Becky.

Michelle Holland

"How rude", says Jo, as she frowns at her.

It isn't long before we are back inside and Daisy heads straight off to the balcony to continue her rabbit duty again. Me and Jacob watch closely with great interest.

"This one is from Mum and Dad", she says, as she hands Jo a square looking parcel.

Jacob immediately rushes over to her and I watch in amazement as he starts to rip off the paper.

'I wouldn't mind having a go at doing that', I say to myself.

"You are such a great help Jacob, thank you. Look Becky, I have a new walking coat. How cool is this?" says Jo, as she holds up her new coat for all of us to see.

"This one is from the boys", Becky tells her, as she hands over a square looking parcel.

I slowly edge closer.

"Would you like to help me open my present too Penny Pops?" Jo asks me.

I go to the opposite side to Jacob and watch him closely. He's got hold of the paper in his teeth and is frantically ripping it off. it off. I copy him and soon there is no paper left.

What great fun that was.

"Look, I have some new walking boots. How awesome is this? I can wear them today and can at last get rid of my old ones, as they have a hole or two or three in them", grins Jo.

Me and Jacob continue to help Jo unwrap her presents. She has a bottle of brandy, some pants, socks, two pairs of combat trousers, her coat and boots, plus over one hundred pounds in money. She seems delighted.

"Now you can open your cards", says Becky, as she hands her a very large pile of square envelopes.

"All except yours", she says to Becky sarcastically.

"Good things come to those who wait", laughs back Becky.

Me and Jacob watch patiently, as Jo reads out the messages on each card.

"I cannot believe how many cards I have", she grins, as Becky gets up and carefully stands them on the shelves around the lounge.

"I'll make us another coffee", Becky replies, once she has placed the last card down.

"Penny Pops, Jacob, go and find your ball", she tells us.

We both head off and within seconds we are back with our balls.

Jo is sitting on the floor.

"Jacob drop", she tells him.

He immediately obliges and I watch as the ball starts to disappear inside the paper. It now looks like a huge ball.

"Find it Jacob", Jo tells him, as she rolls it across the lounge.

Jacob goes into a complete frenzy once he gets hold of it, continuously ripping all the paper off until his ball reappears.

"Well done Jacob", she tells him.

"Do you want to play too Penny Pops?" she asks me.

I think I might just do that, as this looks great fun.

"Come on. Push your ball to me", she tells me.

I focus on my ball, as it begins to disappear inside an enormous amount of paper.

"Find it Penny Pops", she tells me, as I get to work.

I pull bits of paper off with my teeth and toss it to the side. I grasp it tightly in between my two front paws and eventually my ball reappears.

"Yay, good job Penny Pops", she tells me.

"What on earth is going on in here?" asks Becky, as she reappears in the lounge.

"We were only playing", grins Jo.

"Just look at the mess, there is shredded paper everywhere", replies Becky, as she slowly turns her head to look around.

"Hey chill out, we are on holiday. I will clear this up in no time", Jo tells her, as she gets up and heads out of the door.

I trot after her and follow her back to the lounge.

She is scooping the paper up and placing it into a large bag.

I jump into action and pick up some of the paper she can't reach and drop it by her side.

"What a great little helper you are", Becky says looking completely surprised.

Jacob gives me a dirty look, but I don't care, I carry on helping Jo.

"When we've finished our coffee, I'll feed the dogs and get washed and dressed. I was thinking about making us a little picnic to take on our walk. What do you think?" continues Becky.

"I think that is a fabulous idea. It would be nice to have a birthday picnic, as I have never had one before. What do you think Jacob and Penny Pops?" Jo asks us.

'Woof', we both reply in unison.

"That's all sorted. I am glad we have your seal of approval", says Jo with a big grin.

Chapter 41

* * *

"Oh Jo. Isn't this just the most beautiful place ever?" Becky says, as we head off down the green field.

"Amazing Becky and thank you so much for organising this. It is an awesome birthday present", Jo replies.

"Daisy. Come here. You are obsessed with those rabbits", Becky says, as Daisy once again stands on her hind legs in search of her new rabbit friends.

"She looks like a meerkat", says Jo laughing loudly, as she takes a photo of her.

"Forty-nine today Jo. I can't believe it, can you?" says Becky, in a very cheeky manner.

"Don't take the mickey Becky, you are not too far behind me", replies Jo.

I love listening to the banter that goes on between the two of them.

"How old is Jacob again?" asks Becky.

"Jacob is four, and Daisy will also be four in November. Penny Pops will be two in November and can you believe that her and Daisy share the same birthday?" Jo says.

"No way. You are kidding me, right?" replies Becky, sounding quite shocked.

"It is true, I promise. I will show you their veterinary certificates later on to prove it to you", smiles Jo.

"How bizarre is that?" says Becky.

I can't believe, I have a birthday date too. I have never had one before. How exciting is this?

"Do you actually know where we are going?" questions Jo.

"Of course, I do. Look I am following the map. Not far from here is a popular mountain. Well to be honest it is a hill made of limestone. The views at the top are said to be incredible across the peak District and I thought it would be the perfect spot for our picnic, trust me", grins Becky.

"Jacob, Penny Pops please come here. I can see cows ahead", calls out Jo.

"I wonder what Daisy will think of them?" queries Becky.

"I am not too sure, but we'll soon find out", laughs Jo.

'Moo', we suddenly hear.

A manure type scent is flying up my nostrils and is making the end of my nose twitch.

"Wow, that is a very strong smell", says Becky, as she tries hard to stop Daisy from standing on her hind legs.

'Woof', shouts Jacob, as he lunges towards the fence, nearly pulling Jo's arm out.

I bark and jump around, as I sternly tell him off.

"Look Jo. There is the hill in the distance, and there is the stream to the right. How stunning is this?" screeches Becky.

"Wow Becky, I bet the view from the top is spectacular. Maybe we can head down to the stream later so the doggies can have a paddle", replies Jo.

'Now I like the sound of this. Maybe I could have a swim?' I smile to myself.

"I think we should stop and have five minutes rest, so the dogs can have some water before we head up the hill", says Becky.

I watch as Jo takes off her rucksack and pours out a bowl of clean fresh water.

Jacob kindly lets me share the bowl with him, whilst Daisy continues to be on rabbit watch.

"Daisy is going to be mentally exhausted by the time we get home. I have never seen her take this much interest in anything before", laughs Jo.

"Right are we all ready to head off to the top of the hill?" asks Becky, once we have all had a drink.

There are so many smells to check out and we can't help but stop on a regular basis. Becky and Jo are very patient and happily let us take our time.

"Phew, this is quite tiring", says Becky, as we nearly reach the top.

"Tell me about it. My back is aching from carrying this heavy rucksack with the drinks in", replies Jo.

"This is truly breath taking", blurts out Becky, as we eventually reach the top.

"I have never seen anything so magical as this", replies Jo, as she starts to take numerous photos.

"Look there is a nice flat area just over there where we can sit and have our picnic. How incredible are the sunrays glistening onto the stream down there? Look" says Becky.

"Sometimes we forget how beautiful our own country is", Jo says, as she takes off her rucksack and plops it down onto the floor.

"If you keep hold of all three dogs Jo, I will unpack our picnic", informs Becky.

Michelle Holland

I watch as Becky starts to unwrap the sandwiches and my eyes light up when I see her pull out a packet of doggie dental sticks.

Saliva starts to drool from my mouth, and it looks to be having the same affect on Jacob, although Daisy is still in her own little world as she takes in these incredible views.

"You didn't think I would forget you three, did you?" grins Becky, as she kindly hands one to each of us.

"Here is some antibacterial gel to put on your hands before you eat", I hear her tell Jo, as I lie down to enjoy my treat.

"My favourite salad sandwiches. These are absolutely delicious, thank you Becky", Jo says.

"You are welcome Jo and tonight we can all enjoy a birthday meal at the pub, possibly followed by a relaxing hour or so in the hot tub. What do you think?" Becky asks.

"I think that sounds like a perfect plan", smiles Jo, as she finishes off her sandwiches.

"Was yours nice too?" Jo asks me.

I look into her eyes and wink.

"Can you believe Penny Pops just winked at me?" says Jo, sounding astounded.

"What does that mean?" asks Becky.

"It means she is communicating with me and is understanding everything I tell her. How awesome is this?" grins Jo.

I just love the way Jo always understands what I am thinking all the time.

"Right, let me pack this lot away and then I will let you open your remaining card", says Becky.

"So, you finally got around to writing it in the end then? Better late than never", laughs Jo.

"Very funny. Oh, and I have one more present for you, if you want it?" she responds.

"Another present? Coolio", blurts out Jo.

"Firstly, I need you to walk that way until you are around six feet away from us all. I want you to sit down, turn your back on us and close your eyes tightly", she instructs Jo.

"Why?" queries Jo.

"Please do as you are told for once Jo", orders Becky.

I am not too sure what is going on, as Jo hands mine and Jacob's leads over to Becky.

"Right go on, do as I have just told you", she instructs once again.

I try to follow Jo, but Becky is firmly holding my lead.

Michelle Holland

"That's it, now sit down and turn around so your back is facing us. Now close your eyes and no peeking", she continues.

I watch as Jo sits down onto the grass and I sigh with relief that she hasn't gone too far away from us.

"Now please stay still whilst I put a bandana onto each of you", whispers Becky, as she leans forward and ties something around my neck.

I keep one eye on Jo and with my other one I closely watch what Becky is getting up to. Jacob and Daisy also have something around their necks too.

"Nearly ready Jo", Becky calls, as I watch her pull out a card from her rucksack.

"Slowly", she tells us, as we all walk towards Jo.

"Jo, please keep your eyes closed until I tell you to open them", says Becky.

"Jacob, Penny, Daisy, sit please", she tells us, and we immediately oblige.

"Jo, turn around slowly, but do not open your eyes until I tell you", she continues.

I watch Jo shuffle around on her bottom to face us and I can see she still has her eyes tightly closed.

"Ok Jo, open your eyes", Becky says, sounding very excited.

I seriously haven't got a clue what is going on.

Jo blinks a few times and then slowly looks at Daisy, Jacob and finally me. Her mouth is wide open, and she is holding one hand up to her mouth. She doesn't seem to be able to speak and I start to feel concerned as tears begin to run down her face.

"Happy birthday Jo", beams Becky.

"Is this for real? Do you really mean it Becky?" cries out Jo.

'What on earth is going on', I wonder, feeling very confused.

"One hundred percent Jo. Penny is now officially a very important member of our family. Penny go and give your Mummy Jo a big kiss", she replies.

I cannot believe what I am hearing. Am I really staying with Jo, Becky, Jacob and Daisy forever? Am I dreaming all of this?

"Come to Mummy, Penny Pops", Jo says to me, in between her tears.

I immediately rush into her open arms and feel like the luckiest dog in the whole world as she wraps them tightly around me.

"Oh Becky, I just adore their bandanas. Where did you get them made? I couldn't believe it when I read the print on them saying happy birthday Mummy. It took me quite a while for it all to sink in and realise what it meant", Jo continues.

"I know, your face was a picture and looking at your surprised reaction made me cry too. Mum helped me make the bandanas", she replies.

"Really? Are Mum and Dad ok with us keeping Penny?" Jo asks.

"Yes, they are one hundred percent behind us. They said every dog deserves a second chance and Penny more than most after what she has been through. They are positive that with the love and time we can give her, just like we did with Jacob, she will turn into a super family dog", beams Becky.

I am finding it hard to take this all in. I'm still not convinced this is just all a dream.

"Oh, by the way Jo, here is your card. You will see when you open it, why I couldn't give it to you this morning", says Becky, as she hands Jo an envelope.

"Let's have a look at this card then Penny Pops", she tells me, as I sit closely by her side.

"Happy birthday to the best Mummy, in the whole wide world", she reads out.

"All our love and licks, Jacob, Daisy and Penny Pops", she continues, with a slightly croaky voice.

I look at Jo and see the tears have started to freely flow from her eyes once again.

I have a lump in my throat and can feel tears slowly running down my face. I look around at Daisy and Becky, they have tears too. I look at Jacob, I think I can see a tear, but he winks at me and then turns his head away.

'It is true. Jo is officially my Mummy and I have my very own forever family at last. How lucky am I?' I cry to myself.

I look directly into Jo's teary eyes.

That warm and fuzzy feeling erupts throughout every part of my body, and in between my tears, I wink at Jo and she winks back.

THE MOTTO OF THIS STORY IS, NEVER GIVE UP ON A RESCUE DOG.

THE END

Printed by Amazon Italia Logistica S.r.l.
Torrazza Piemonte (TO), Italy